Fernando —

The Greatest Job You Never Thought Of

How Anyone Can Find Career Satisfaction
and Financial Independence in Sales

Frank Felker

To the BEST

CSR in the

world!

The Greatest Job You Never Thought Of

How Anyone Can Find Career Satisfaction and Financial Independence in Sales
by Frank Felker

Published by:
Powerhouse Publishing
9538 Old Keene Mill Road, #324
Burke, Virginia 22015, USA

orders@powerhousepublishing.com
http://www.powerhousepublishing.com
866-390-1945 (phone/fax)

Unattributed quotations by Frank Felker.

ISBN paperback ed.   0-9759400-3-1
ISBN hardcover ed.   0-9759400-0-7
ISBN PDF ed.   0-9759400-1-5
ISBN audio ed.   0-9759400-2-3

First paperback printing January 2005
Printed in the United States of America

Library of Congress Control Number: 2004096272

Felker, Frank
The greatest job you never thought of, how anyone can find career satisfaction and financial independence in sales
1st paperback ed.
ISBN   0-9759400-3-1

The Greatest Job
You Never Thought Of

How Anyone Can Find Career Satisfaction
and Financial Independence in Sales

Frank Felker

POWER
HOUSE

PUBLISHING

Burke · Virginia

POWER
HOUSE
PUBLISHING

Dedication

This book is dedicated to two groups of people whose faith in me made my success as a salesman possible; my family and the team at Procraft of Virginia.

My wife Lori, mother Toby, children Jimmy and Jessica, and siblings Lex and Sally, have always stood by me and supported me in good times and bad. Without them nothing I have ever accomplished would have been possible, and nothing I will ever attempt be meaningful.

Greg Deathridge, Melinda Hawks and Randy Carter at Procraft of Virginia saw the potential for sales success in me that I probably didn't even see myself, and gave me the opportunity, training, resources, support and - most importantly - the leads I needed to become a top producer.

Acknowledgments

A great number of people assisted me in the preparation of this book.

First and foremost I want to thank John Gorman for his moral support, creative input, proofreading and prodding. Bob Sullivan, my longtime friend and sales mentor, also was instrumental in the creation of this book.

Thanks also to John Paine and Jack Hartman for lending their true-life stories, and to Tony Mayo and Mike Weiner for lending their names and reputations to my promotional efforts.

My gratitude also goes out to Cliff Claggett, Andrew Lee, Jon Baker, Andrew Clore, Eric Anderson, Alan MacDonald, Mike Hensley, Don Park, Frank Amory, Doug Lewis, Roberto, Michelle, Melissa, Ricardo, Lorenzo Greene, and all my other compatriots at Procraft of Virginia for everything they taught me.

Last but not least I must acknowledge all of my customers, without whose support this story would never have been written.

Disclaimer

This book is designed to provide information about the subject matter covered. It is sold with the understanding that the publisher and author are not engaged in rendering legal, accounting or other professional services. If legal or other expert assistance is required, the services of a competent professional should be sought.

It is not the purpose of this book to reprint all of the information that is otherwise available to job seekers and/or salespeople but to complement, simplify and supplement other texts.

Transitioning to a career in sales is not a get-rich-quick scheme. Anyone who chooses a career in sales must be dedicated, hard-working and willing to persevere in the face of adversity if they wish to succeed.

Every effort has been made to make this book as complete and accurate as possible. However, there may be mistakes both typographical and in content within this text. Therefore, this book should only be used as a general guide and not as the ultimate source of job seeking and

The Greatest Job
You Never Thought Of

How Anyone Can Find Career Satisfaction
and Financial Independence in Sales

Frank Felker

Burke · Virginia

POWER
HOUSE
PUBLISHING

Table of Contents

Chapter 3: The Sales Skill Set

Chapter 4: The Sales Cycle

Chapter 5: Choosing The Right Product and Company

Chapter 6: Selling Yourself

Conclusion: Now It's Your Turn

Introduction:
How I Came To Be A Salesman

Like many of you reading these words, I never saw myself as a salesperson.

Some people come to sales from a previous career in the military, in computers, in management, even from the factory floor. I was an entrepreneur.

My mother started a printing business when I was fifteen. I worked there part-time through high school and college and, after receiving a degree in economics, ran the shop for fourteen years, growing it to over $1 million in revenue before selling out to our general manager.

After the print shop was sold I tried my hand at a number of entrepreneurial endeavors. I published a newsletter targeting the printing industry, started a printing-oriented dot-com and created a home-based multimedia production company. Unfortunately, none of these ventures provided the level of income I had enjoyed at the printing company, where, in my best years, I earned a healthy six-figure income with health benefits, a company car and all the other perks that accrue to a business owner. And the lifestyle I had created during those higher-flying years began dragging my family and I down in debt. Out of desperation I started looking for a "real job,"something I had never done before.

My job hunt strategy was to pursue two tracks simultaneously: 1) A career-oriented search focused on executive-level marketing and/or management positions; 2) A short-term oriented search for a high paying sales job that would quickly get my financial world back in order. If I found an executive job that I liked –great: search over. On the other hand, if I found a sales position first, I would use the flexible schedule most sales jobs offer to continue my hunt for the job I thought I really wanted.

While I had never been a salesperson, I knew a bit about sales jobs having hired and managed salespeople in the printing and dot-com businesses. And I knew a number of successful salespeople in printing, real estate and other industries, who made seemingly obscene amounts of money.

I call sales "The World's Most Valuable Profession" because my training in economics has shown me that resources flow to their highest-value use. This is almost a law of nature. With this in mind, the only way that salespeople can possibly earn what they are paid is by generating huge amounts of value. That is just what they do.

As an entrepreneur, I had done a bit of selling myself though none of it as a "salesman." Frankly, I thought that was beneath me and, I don't mind admitting, the idea of trying to earn a living solely from sales commissions frightened me. I know I am not alone in those feelings and will speak to both the stigma surrounding "salesmen" and risk aversion further in *Chapter 2: Why Not A Career in Sales?*

Back to my job hunt: I spent hours every Sunday combing through the classifieds looking under Advertising, Association Management, Marketing, Management and Sales. Funny thing though: Sales always had the most listings – by a long shot! I created separate resumes and cover letters for the various positions and developed short email messages for responding to ads. I also posted my resumes to the various web-based jobs sites like Monster, HotJobs, etc.

My first surprise was how long it took for people to get back to me regarding executive position postings. I was applying to so many similar positions that, by the time I received a response, I often couldn't remember the specifics of the company calling me. Weeks would go by – even to get a "thanks-but-no-thanks" letter.

On the other hand I found that responses from sales postings were almost always a great deal faster. Apparently when a company is looking to hire salespeople it's because they want to increase sales, and that's something that has a higher level of urgency associated with it.

I went on a number of interviews for executive positions, even making it to the final three candidates out of over 50 applicants for the position of Director of Marketing for a regional credit union. But none of the jobs offered me the kind of money I was looking for. (I think I lost the credit union gig because I told them my starting salary requirements were between $85,000 and $100,000) What those jobs did offer however was a steady paycheck, strong benefits packages and the "prospect" of upward career mobility. That's if you get the job, and I hadn't gotten one yet.

Then one day I received a phone call from a sales manager who was opening a new office in my area for a home improvement company called Procraft of Virginia. I had responded to an ad they had placed in the newspaper for in-home salespeople. The sales manager had seen my resume and wanted to talk to me – even though I had no direct experience in his industry. The job would involve making presentations to homeowners across their kitchen table trying to convince them to purchase Liquid Siding: in essence is a permanent exterior paint job. Was I interested?

In a word, no, I wasn't. I had responded to the ad without knowing exactly what was involved because the commission plan outlined sounded attractive. The very thought of pitching people in their homes horrified me. I knew nothing about construction, paint, home improvement or in-home sales. Also, the position was pure commission – no base salary, no draw, no nothing.

Worst of all, the job involved what's known in the sales trade as a one-call close. You either sell the job during your first visit or you almost certainly will not sell it at all. What did I figure my odds were of convincing a high enough percentage of people to sign-up for projects costing thousands of dollars the very first time I met them? Especially when I had no idea what I was talking about! Not good.

So why would anyone even consider this job? Because of the income potential. Without getting into the details of the commission structure, I can tell you that I knew enough about sales incentives to immediately see that a top producer could earn $200,000 or more per year with this company. I also knew that my region (metropolitan Washington, DC) was one of the wealthiest in the country and that I would be one of the first salespeople with access to that virgin territory.

The commission structure provided that up to half of your earnings would be paid the same week you signed the customer, with the balance coming when the job was completed in 4-6 weeks. This meant that I could begin bringing in money almost immediately – provided that I could sell the stuff.

To make a long story short, I took the job. And while I started off very poorly, not closing a deal until my fourteenth appointment, within three months I was one of the top salesmen in the company. I was named Rookie of the Year and runner-up Salesman of the Year. In the final six months of my first year I earned over $80,000 in commissions with better than $20,000 coming in one month alone.

How I was able to make that incredible transition is the essence of this book. My experience has led me to the conclusion that anyone can find a similar level of financial success and personal satisfaction in sales – provided that they are sufficiently motivated and committed, find a product and company they really believe in, that offers the right commission plan, and have access to the necessary resources.

That is the purpose for this book: to give you a new perspective on sales as a profession, and to help you find a great sales job that will make you more money than you may have thought possible while having a lot of fun – and give you the tools to land and succeed at that job.

Sales is not easy – neither is any other profession, certainly not any that pay as well. But it is not impossible either. The top echelon of sales is not the domain of some elite group of smoothies who know how to fast-talk their way into a person's wallet. It is where great listeners, who represent a product they really believe in, solve problems for important people – their customers.

Read on and learn how anyone can succeed at sales. Even you!

Frank Felker

Chapter 1:
The Magic of Sales,
The World's Most
Valuable Profession

There are obstacles to sales career success and we will discuss them head-on in the next chapter. But before I get to any negativity, I want to talk about all of the great reasons to become a salesperson.

Number of Jobs Available

I believe there are more sales jobs than any other single skill category. Sales offers the largest number of entry-level positions on Monster.com, with over 23% of all such positions. CareerBuilder.com offers over 60,000 sales positions. Typing the word "sales" into the jobs search engine on WashingtonPost.com immediately yields the maximum number of responses (500) for any query.

If you look in the classified section of any newspaper in America you are likely to find more listings under the category of Sales than any other. Sure, there may be whole sections for Health Care and/or Technology Jobs, but within those sections are a wide variety of job names and descriptions, each requiring a specific set of skills, education or career background. Unlike the Sales category, you can't just decide to leave your job as a Medical Office Administrator and apply to an opening for a Surgical Technician.

Unimportance of Previous Experience

On the other hand, a successful salesperson can apply for openings in pharmaceuticals, automobile retailing, financial services, commercial real estate or any number of other disparate industries. Certainly product knowledge is fundamental to long-term sales success in a given industry, and we will discuss that in detail in *Chapter 3: The Sales Skill Set.* But product knowledge is something your employer can and will teach you and that you can learn more about on your own or on the job.

Your skills as a salesperson are more critical and, for the most part, will transfer seamlessly from one industry to the next. When looking to make your first move into a sales position, specific product knowledge is not critical.

For example: the first listing I clicked on when running the WashingtonPost.com search mentioned above yielded the following employer's slant on how much product knowledge their ideal sales candidate needed:

We are more interested in general drive, organizational skills and enthusiasm than in specific computer product knowledge or prior work experience. We can teach the rest.

I did not make that up; it came straight from their ad.

The point is that there are many tens of thousands of lucrative sales positions available today, there always have been and there always will be. Learn to be a successful salesperson, and you'll never find yourself out of work for long.

Meritocracy

I once heard the color analyst on a football broadcast describe the NFL as a democracy, where everyone has an equal chance to succeed and politics play little part in career success. Well, his thought was correct but his vocabulary was a bit off. Democracy means that each person has an equal say, one person, one vote. What he was referring to is a meritocracy, where each person's value is determined by what they produce, what they merit, not who they know within the organization.

The same is true with sales. If you have had problems with office politics in the past you'll love being a salesperson. I'm not going to tell you that there are no politics in sales – put any three people together in a room and within five minutes you'll have a political hierarchy. What I am saying is that you can climb high on the totem pole without having to kiss anyone's butt. Just go out and sell.

This is one of my favorite features of the sales game. Work hard, develop yourself, be persistent and consistent and you'll not only make a lot of money, you'll also earn status and respect within your company. Race, religion, background, all mean nothing. Sales is a meritocracy.

High Income

At most jobs, no matter how hard you work you still make the same amount of money. Your annual performance evaluation may or may not yield a raise and, unless you're a federal employee, you're unlikely to see any cost-of-living increases. In sales your income is only limited by your skills and work ethic. Not all sales positions offer the same income potential, but many have no limit on the amount of money you can make.

I know a mortgage loan officer who makes over $1 million per year. An acquaintance of mine from the printing industry pulls down almost 8% of the $10 million book of business he has built over the past 20-plus years as a salesperson. (In case you wondering that's almost $800,000 per year and, yes, I have seen his pay stubs.) Top automobile salespeople earn $150,000 or more annually. Insurance sales can generate six-figure residual income streams in 2-3 years. Successful radio ad salespeople often earn over $250,000. I could go on and on with examples from pharmaceutical sales, software, farm equipment, you name it.

Don't Need That Much?

Does all of this talk about people making $100,000 or more make you nervous? Perhaps your goal is more modest and you either think that you don't deserve or wouldn't know what to do with $8,000 or more every month.

Maybe you just like the idea of a sales job because of the career certainty, schedule flexibility, meritocracy and other benefits it offers. Maybe you'd like working shorter hours – or fewer days – and still make more than you can in your current job.

That's great! Don't make yourself miserable chasing after something you don't want. Your internal thermostat probably won't let you get there anyway. On the other hand, don't be surprised if you start making that kind of dough in spite of yourself. We'll talk more about finding a sales job that matches your preferences in *Chapter 5: Choosing The Right Product and Company For You.*

Flexibility and Perks

Most sales jobs are inherently flexible from a daily schedule standpoint. Show up at your appointments, close the right percentage of deals, submit your paperwork correctly and you won't have anyone looking over your shoulder or expecting you to be at the office at 8:30 every morning.

All management is going to look at is your numbers. Keep the numbers up and everybody's happy. Not that I'm understating the importance or difficulty of meeting your sales goals, it's just that, if you do, everything else sort of takes care of itself.

The trick from a scheduling standpoint is structuring yourself. You must make time for prospecting, follow-up, paperwork and a variety of other things without someone else telling you when to do what where. You won't have to punch a clock but you will have to manage time.

Successful salespeople are also given a bit of slack in other areas such as vacation scheduling, automobile allowances, travel and entertainment budgets, etc. Many companies will pay for their salespeople's country club memberships so they can entertain clients on the links. Company cars, cell phones, vacation trips (for winning sales contests) and other perks are commonplace.

Entrepreneurial Upside Without The Risk

As I mentioned in the introduction to this book, I have been a career entrepreneur. To many people that sounds great: be your own boss, run your own business, set your own rules. It does have its advantages, but it also carries with it a great deal of risk.

Depending on the business you operate, you may have a significant amount of overhead, retail, office or warehouse space, insurance and so forth. For most businesses payroll is their biggest expense category, and meeting it every payday can be a nightmare. In the printing business I made payroll every Friday for fourteen years (that's 728 consecutive weeks, but who's counting?). In the dot-com business I wasn't so lucky and many people, including myself, were irreparably harmed. I wouldn't wish that experience on you.

Business owners also have to hire, fire and manage people. They worry about inventory, signage, marketing, finance, administration, production, delivery, insurance subcontractors, OSHA, the INS, the fire marshal and a whole host of other things. Some business owners do make a lot of money, but, take my word for it: they earn it.

In sales you get many of the rewards of entrepreneurship with almost none of the hassles. You are in fact running your own business, setting your own goals and schedule, managing your time and resources. You often have an unlimited upside earnings potential but none of the risk that the business owner assumes. Other than yourself you have no payroll worries, you're not responsible for production or delivery, overhead is not your concern and keeping George in accounting off the sauce is somebody else's problem.

When I first started in my sales job, I almost felt guilty about the lack of responsibility I was shouldering. I got over it. There is an old adage in sales that "Nothing happens until somebody sells something," and brother I was making things happen. I decided that was enough for me to focus on.

There is of course one risk that you assume: the risk that you won't sell anything. But, if you owned the whole business, that would be just one of your worries.

Small Business Training Ground

If my warnings above have not dispelled your dreams of business ownership, I can recommend no better training ground for aspiring entrepreneurs than the School of Salesmanship. Most business owners I have known are great at and passionate about what they do, but they don't know beans about sales or marketing. Those who come from a background in sales ramp up their businesses much more quickly and make a lot more money, on average, than those who don't.

I will give you a quick example.

In the mid-1980s, two printing salesmen purchased a storefront print shop nearby to ours. Prior to their arrival the company had gone through two sets of family owners with no real growth or profitability over the course of almost ten years. That changed very quickly after "The Two Jerrys" arrived.

Being that they had their own butts on the line, The Jerrys went out and sold like there was no tomorrow. Non-compete agreements they had signed with their previous employer prevented them from bringing in business from their existing clients so they went out and got all new customers in the first twelve months, then added their previous book of business in the second year. Sales doubled in the first six months and just kept climbing from there.

The Jerrys knew very little about production, management or administration but were smart enough to bring in people who did to keep the books and run the plant. Within a year they moved to an industrial park and three years after that purchased a large building where they remain to this day. They have generated tens of millions of dollars in revenue and their only regret was buying an existing business rather than starting from scratch.

I could give you any number of other examples, but the essence of my experience in this area is that a savvy salesperson has a higher probability of succeeding in a given business than a savvy production person or administrator – provided that the salesperson-turned-business owner can keep their eye on the prize and recognize that production is as important as sales.

I am aware of other stories where a salesperson took over an existing business and ran it into the ground because they couldn't be bothered with boring stuff like bookkeeping and delivery. If you're not going to take your business seriously, no previous training will save you.

A Few Real-Life Examples of The Magic of Sales

As I was writing this book I began talking to salespeople, asking how they happened to come into sales and how it has worked out for them. The stories I heard were remarkable and, if I continue to gather them in sufficient numbers, may serve as the grist for another book on the sales profession.

Story One: I spoke with an insurance agent we'll call "Joe" who had previously worked for the federal government for twenty years – most of that time at the Social Security Administration. One day, while still a federal worker, Joe met an insurance agent who persuaded Joe that his experience with retirement benefits made him a perfect candidate to sell life insurance and financial planning services.

After taking an early retirement buy-out offer from the government, our hero studied for and received his insurance license and began prospecting small business owners and real estate agents. While he didn't enjoy cold calling, he developed a reputation of providing honest answers to people – never lying or being pushy – and, as a result, his referral business began to grow. People knew they could call Joe for straight answers without the fear of being "sold."

While his slow and steady approach required several years to really pay off (remember he had his retirement income), today he is pulling in very strong residual income (he wouldn't tell me how much), living in a resort community and doing no outbound marketing whatsoever. Most of his existing policies just keep rolling over year after year and his client base keeps sending him more referrals. Basically he just answers the phone. That's good work if you can get it!

Story Two: Among other interests, I am an amateur musician, songwriter and producer. I like to wander through music stores, window shopping and learning about the latest technology. One day while visiting the largest local music shop, I began visiting with a sales guy in the professional audio department.

This man we'll call "Tom" had previously been a geologist for a government contractor, working on testing and remediation of soil and water which had been polluted by faulty underground petroleum tanks of the kind buried beneath every gas station. One day Tom read that the first President Bush had signed a bill eliminating the regulation of environmental issues by individual states and creating a very lenient set of federal standards for the states to follow. Before he knew it Tom was out of work – in spite of having a degree in geology and years of work experience behind him.

Tom moved to California to receive formal training in audio engineering, a field he had always been interested in. After many months of training and tens of thousands of dollars in tuition, he learned that after graduation he would still have to start at the bottom of the ladder, working long hours and earning minimum wage, if he wanted to get a job at any of the major recording studios in Los Angeles. Not an appealing prospect at age 40.

A growing regional music store looking for salespeople got Tom's name from the workshop company where he had trained and offered him a position selling pro audio equipment in Los Angeles at the company's flagship store on Sunset Boulevard. Ten months later, when the music store chain expanded to the east coast, he moved back east to be closer to his roots, having grown up and attended college in West Virginia.

Today Tom is earning more than twice what he did as a geologist. He does no prospecting, cold calling or travel, commutes one mile from his home to the music store, works five days per week and sometimes only three hours per day. Having made a great living from sales for years, he now says he could never imagine doing any other type of work, whether it be a desk job, geologist or whatever. He loves helping people and his down-to-earth, knowledgeable approach has made Tom the top salesman in his store.

Story Three: A customer I signed-up at Procraft currently earns over $1 million per year and lives in a home which is 120 feet wide and nearly 50 feet tall. How do I know the dimensions of his house? I had to measure it to give him a price!

When my sales manager, Randy Carter, and I went to sign the contracts with this customer we'll call "Mr. Johnson," Randy asked him what he did for a living. His answer lasted over 90 minutes but boiled down to a case of someone giving sales a chance when nothing else seemed to be working.

Mr. Johnson grew up in the Shenandoah Valley of Virginia in a small town called Mount Jackson which is adjacent to I-81, about 75 miles southwest of Washington, DC. Barely graduating from high school, he never even considered attending college and began working a variety of low-paying jobs for Virginia Power, the electrical utility.

One day his wife suggested that he speak to her uncle about a position the uncle had open for someone to sell heavy equipment in central Pennsylvania. Our hero traveled north to take a sales aptitude test and was surprised to find that his was the highest score the company had ever seen. Suddenly, a young man who had always been told that he couldn't do anything right found something he could excel at.

Mr. Johnson did very well at the heavy equipment company and several years later was approached by a friend who had an idea about distributing fresh mushrooms to restaurants and needed someone who knew how to sell. Johnson didn't know anything about the food service industry and thought the idea of being in the mushroom business sounded silly. But he found the upside potential in the story his friend told to be sufficiently compelling to strike out in a new direction.

The two entrepreneurs got up early every morning, purchased fresh mushrooms at farmers markets and sold them to as many fancy restaurants as they could find – charging a premium price and delivering a premium product. Over time they expanded to supplying grocery stores and institutional food companies.

He eventually bought out his partner and now runs the entire business single-handedly from his palatial home. He doesn't even have a secretary! Just a phone, fax machine and the Internet. Where his sales skills had originally allowed him to establish relationships with the growers and the buyers - with his employees doing the pick-ups, deliveries and paperwork - he now orchestrates the entire process in just a few hours per day using contracted trucking companies. What a country!

Story Four: You may have heard of Bill Porter, the salesman for Watkins Products who was born with cerebral palsy. If anyone's life story proves that there are no barriers to sales success other than commitment and hard work, it's Bill Porter's.

With the support and encouragement of his mother, Bill walked miles everyday, selling a variety of products from a catalog door-to-door. In spite of his handicap he also delivered all of the products to his customers when they came in – until his business grew so large that he had to hire an assistant.

Bill's life story is well told in a made-for-TV movie entitled "Door To Door" which appeared originally on Turner Network Television and is now available on video for rent or purchase. The story was co-written by William H. Macy (remember "Fargo"?) who also stars in the lead role. Anytime someone tries to tell me that they "can't" sell, I suggest they watch that movie and call me back to explain what's slowing them down. "Can't" and "won't" (or "don't want to") are not synonymous.

The Bottom Line

As you can see, a career in sales has a lot going for it. Not everyone will see or reach for the opportunity, but those that do, and commit themselves to success, are richly rewarded.

Chapter 2:
Why Not A Career in Sales?

There is a long-running dispute regarding whether anyone can become a successful salesperson or if "special skills" are required. A recent article in a prestigious sales management trade magazine cautioned sales managers against hiring novices because "the nature of sales has become more consultative, requiring complicated skills that most newbies don't have – and don't realize they need."

Puh-leeze. Sales has always involved listening, finding out where the pain is, using your knowledge to craft a solution and persuading the customer to prove they agree with you by writing a check. Which skills are required today which weren't needed previously?

I have also read where sales management consultants have cautioned their clients against hiring people who haven't the right personality traits to become a top performer. My response to this is that only a small fraction of any population has the innate traits required to become a top performer in any given field, from sales to the National Football League. There aren't many Michael Vicks, Payton Mannings or Ray Lewises available, but there are still almost 2,000 men earning a great living as professional football players.

The same is true with sales. While some top performers will earn from $250,000 to $1 million or more annually, there are tens of thousands of "lesser talents" making $75,000 to $125,000 with their more limited innate skills – skills that can be developed and improved over time.

One difference between sales and football is that you can choose to make a living in sales no matter your height, weight, speed in the 40, background, age or other personal attributes. I once heard Brian Tracy, the personal development guru, say that he had known people "who couldn't lead silent prayer in a phone booth" who became very successful salespeople over time. I'm with Brian on that one.

As for why people decide not to choose sales as a career; I believe there are five primary reasons, all of which can be boiled down to a single word: fear.

The Stigma

If we were to survey people's reaction to the word "salesman" we would probably find that a majority of respondents would be negatively predisposed. The image of the pushy salesman is reinforced (ironically enough) in commercials and through television shows and films.

We've all heard jokes made about used car salesmen and seen movies like *Tin Men* and *Glen Garry Glen Ross*. I once even had a homeowner say to me during a presentation "I don't want to say you're a salesman, but I guess you are." He guessed right!

I don't want to dismiss this fear because it was a very real one for me – at first. For many weeks I didn't tell most of my friends and acquaintances what I was doing for a living. Many were executives and successful entrepreneurs whose opinions I valued. All were surprised when they did find out and most were very supportive. It became clear that people who did somehow think less of me in this job were people I didn't want to associate with anyway. I got over it and ended up writing a book to tell the whole world!

The fact is that while there are some bad apples in the sales game – and every other game – most successful salespeople make the big bucks because they bring a lot of value to a lot of people. They listen when their customers tell them where they need help and bring them the solution quickly at an affordable price. The world today is being brought closer together because of free trade, and salespeople are the catalyst of commerce.

If you believe in the value of your product and the ethics of the company you represent, then you have nothing to be ashamed of and a great deal to be proud of. And it may be that dealing with this (perceived or real) stigma is one of the things salespeople do to earn the big bucks!

Risk Aversion

The next fear people have about sales is risk: they don't like the idea of not having a guaranteed paycheck coming in. Sales commissions fluctuate, with some checks in the five-figure range and some weeks bringing nothing at all. I once opened a pay envelope expecting to find over $2,000 and instead found $89.23. Another time I didn't think I'd get a check at all and was surprised to get over $4,000 in commission and bonus. My best week was just under $9,000, my worst was zero. That's more variance than a lot of people's constitutions can take.

None of this was monkey business; it's just the vagaries of commission-only sales. Every dime I earned was paid to me, just sometimes sooner than other times depending upon when projects were completed, customers paid up and their checks cleared. If you absolutely have to know what your paycheck is going to be on Friday, this field is going to drive you crazy. And, even if *you* can tolerate it, your spouse may feel differently.

But, in case you weren't aware, let me let you in on a little secret: there's no such thing as a guaranteed paycheck. If you or someone you know hasn't lost their job after ten years or more of loyal service to the same company then you must be living in an isolation booth. As James Thurber once said, "There is no safety in numbers, or in anything else."

The risk of income variation in sales just operates on a shorter time horizon. As a salaried employee you may not be worrying right now about losing your current job because you see that as something which "may" happen "in the future." That thinking falls down when the future is now and your options for quickly replacing your previous income are limited because the factors that squeezed you out are affecting everyone and every company in your industry. If you think it can't happen to you, think again.

In the sales world you may have a bad week or month here or there, but the odds are that it's just a prelude to a string of deals that are right around the corner. As long as you keep plowing ahead making presentations, the law of averages evens everything out.

If you come to the conclusion that either the product or company you are representing is the reason your sales have gone sour, then your sales experience gives you a great entrée to other jobs being advertised, and your flexible schedule gives you the time you need to spiff up your resume and go out on employment interviews.

Any investor worth their salt is aware of the risk-return relationship: the higher the risk the greater the potential return. The difference between buying a penny stock and starting a career as a salesperson is that you can directly impact your probability of success and will see the upside very quickly. You're not just waiting around to see what will happen.

Lack of Structure

As a lifelong entrepreneur this was not a problem for me, but many people coming from more traditional career paths fear the significant reduction of structure that a sales job entails. If you are used to – and comfortable with – driving the same route (or taking the same bus) to the same job for the same hours every day, doing the same thing for the same boss for the same pay, you may have difficulty switching to sales.

In sales you will be meeting new people, driving or flying to new locations, listening to new sets of needs, developing new strategies and closing new deals every day. Just like any job, your sales position will occasionally remind you of the movie *Groundhog Day*. But, for the most part, you will find that things are more different than similar on a daily basis.

You challenge will be structuring yourself. Setting goals, prioritizing, sticking to your self-created schedule, resisting distractions, being persistent and consistent – all are traits of successful salespeople. While you may not be accustomed to many of these behavior patterns, they can be learned. Most of them boil down to a single factor: self-discipline. If you aren't disciplined – and aren't interested in changing – you won't succeed in sales. On the other hand, self-discipline is a trait that can be learned and developed if one is motivated to improve.

Fear of Rejection

This is a biggie: tolerating that ugly word "NO." Nobody likes to hear "I'm not interested," "Not right now," "I don't have time to talk to you," "Can't you take a hint?" or the thousand other ways that salespeople get rejected.

It's human nature to try be agreeable (for most people at least) and to want other people agree with you. Putting yourself in a position where you know that six (or more) out of every ten times you present people are going to disagree with you is hard for many people to deal with. But in the sales world this skill is essential.

Some people call it "having a thick skin" or "letting it roll off your back." My approach was to acknowledge my feelings of rejection when they occurred but not dwell on them. I would immediately begin thinking about my next call and how I could improve to avoid the same outcome. I would also reflect back on some of my biggest successes and how many of them came in situations where I thought I was going to lose the sale but didn't. Finally, the purely logical part of my brain would calculate how much closer that last "no" got me to my next "yes" via the law of averages.

This is not to say that it doesn't hurt, because it can. It just hurts less and less each time as you begin to recognize that it is nothing personal, just part of your job and a big part of why salespeople make the big bucks. The rejections also make the successes that much sweeter, much like the joy of welcoming Spring after a nasty Winter.

Talking to Strangers

I once knew a motivational sales consultant in the printing industry named Sean McArdle. Sean bills himself as The $100 Million Printing Salesman because of the success he has had in the field. He does consulting, presents seminars and produced an audio series called *The Art & Science of Printing Sales*. I don't agree with everything Sean has to say, but there is one area where I feel he is directly on target.

In a section in his audio series on "Call Reluctance" which relates to salespeople's resistance to making calls to prospects with whom they have not yet developed a relationship, Sean would ask his audience to return to their childhood, where our most basic fears are born and fostered. Sean would ask his audience,

> *"What is the number one thing your parents always told you not to do as a child? Talk to strangers.*
>
> *Even if you weren't kidnapped, talking to a stranger was one of the worst things any child could possibly do.*
>
> *And if you did do something wrong as a child, what was the worst possible way to do it? On purpose.*
>
> *You might get away with a misdeed if you could convince your parents it was an accident, but doing it on purpose, well, that's something else entirely.*
>
> *The problem with sales for most people is that it involves Talking To Strangers On Purpose."*

Isn't that a great summation?

I believe this idea of Talking To Strangers On Purpose is one of the biggest fears most people have when they consider a sales position. It's human nature to fear the unknown and what could be more fearsome or unknowable than a human being? *What will they think of me? What if they don't like me? What if they yell at me or just disrespectfully blow me off? What if I mispronounce their name, belch or say something I shouldn't?*

Hey, any or all of these things can and will happen. The strange thing is that none of them preclude you from making a sale – unless you let them. I could fill another entire book with nothing but anecdotes of how I did or said the wrong thing but recovered sufficiently to close the deal. It happens to everyone and can actually help you by making you appear less of a threat to your prospect. Don't forget – they're afraid of you too!

There is also the overriding fear that the person you are about to meet will be a complete jerk, someone you just don't want to have to deal with. This does happen but only rarely. In the hundreds of sales calls I've made I have met only a handful of people who were out-and-out S.O.B.s. And a couple of them were just acting that way to see how I would react.

Most of the people I have met have been wonderful. In fact, meeting new people is one of the things I like best about sales. This was a surprise to me because I have never been the most socially nimble individual. I'm usually a wallflower at parties and, in the past at least, avoided making conversation with people I didn't know while shopping or elsewhere.

As a salesperson I met people of every color and creed, from every walk of life, every income level, single people, families, young, old – you name it. People told me stories of their travels and travails, the people they have met and the things they have done. I saw couples who had been married for decades who were still are madly in love, children and parents interacting – the whole web of human existence.

At Procraft I also found that meeting people in their home gives you a chance to know them on a deeper level than if you were presenting to them at their office. You get to see how they live and whom they live with. And they feel more comfortable opening up to you because they're on their own turf.

In short this is a fear you can and should overcome. You are not a child anymore, so you don't have to worry about being kidnapped – or what your parents will think when they find out you disobeyed their wishes. Your product is a great one that everyone would want if they only knew more about it. So you're doing these strangers a great service by talking to them – on purpose!

By the way, for more wisdom from Sean McArdle, visit his web site at PrintingSales.com

Chapter 3:
The Sales Skill Set

I have stated several times throughout this book that I believe anyone can earn a great living as a successful salesperson, provided they are sufficiently motivated and committed and have access to the proper resources. That statement makes no mention of the skills or talents that each individual brings to the equation, and for good reason.

Talents are personal abilities you are born with which give you a huge head start on others who weren't so blessed. Skills are personal abilities you have created or improved through training and practice. While you may never exceed the ability of a gifted athlete, musician, actor or artist, you can emulate the processes used by superstar salespeople. You may not have been born with their talents, but you can develop the skills they use.

Another important point is that, while all the skills listed below are important to sales success, the absence of one or two does not ensure failure. There has never been a salesperson who was strong in every area. All had to compensate for weaknesses in certain areas with strength in others.

For example: you may not be the most gifted conversationalist, but if you possess exceptional product knowledge, are utterly dependable and completely committed to serving your customers' needs, you will find a great deal of success in sales. On the flip side, you may be completely new to your product line, can't find your way around a new city and haven't gotten your cell phone service started, but yet be so engaging and persuasive as to start bringing in business your first week.

Everybody's situation is different. Play to your skills. Recognize your weaknesses and create a plan to develop yourself in those areas. No two successful salespeople approach their jobs the same way or with the same skill set. Do the best you can from the start and improve over time.

The list below is not in any particular order of importance, except for the first two items: Belief; and Motivation & Commitment. Without these skills securely in your quiver you are destined to fail. With them nothing can stop you.

Belief

Belief, Faith, Trust, Certainty – whatever you want to call it, if you want to succeed in sales you have to have it. Belief in the product or service you are representing and the exceptional value it provides to customers. Faith that your customers will feel as good about making the purchase a week later as they did the day you signed them up. Trust that your company will back the claims you make regarding quality and customer service. And certainty that your customers will act as references for you going forward.

We can become suspicious when we read words like Belief, Faith, etc. It's easy to assume that the author is just feeding us a line of bull in an attempt to get us jazzed up. That may often be the case, but I can assure you that here it is not. I am telling you what I have seen work with my own two eyes.

It's as simple as this: if you believe that your product is great and that you are bringing enormous value to your customers, that belief will be broadcast in everything you do. You will get up every morning ready to go out and bring good stuff to total strangers. You will look forward to each appointment. Your prospects will sense the confidence and enthusiasm you have about your offering and want to become a part of it. Every time you close a deal you'll feel great about it, knowing that you have done well not only for yourself and your firm but for your customer as well, delivering value to them in excess of the price they paid.

On the other hand, if you think your offering stinks, the company you work for is completely disorganized and inept – or even worse, a den of thieves – and that all you're doing is stealing money from the people who are stupid enough to be talked into buying your product, then *those* emotions are likely to be reflected in everything you do.

You will be less than thrilled to greet each morning. You will be reluctant to call on prospects, your presentations will include half-truths and your responses to questions will be evasive. Prospects will sense your unease and want to disassociate from you. Your sales production will be minimal and your home life abysmal.

At Procraft of Virginia, my belief in the unique attributes of Liquid Siding was critical to my success. Initially I didn't even know the difference between latex and oil-based paint so I started asking lots of questions of my co-workers, sales manager and the owner of the company. The company provided training and I did a great deal of research on my own through the Internet.

I learned that Liquid Siding was a unique combination of coating products developed by Kryton, an international manufacturer based in Vancouver, British Columbia. Over the preceding thirty years Kryton had developed a worldwide reputation with governments and multinational construction companies for providing coating systems and additives that far surpassed the competition in appearance and durability. Their products were always the best – and the most expensive.

This commitment to quality – of providing a premium product and requiring a premium return – was directly in alignment with my lifetime approach to business. I've never been one to try to attract customers with discounts because I've found that customers who come to you for the lowest price will leave you for the same reason. Kryton's philosophy was working so well that they now had manufacturing plants on every continent except Antarctica and had just opened their newest and largest facility in mainland China.

The more I learned the more convinced I became that Liquid Siding truly was the best product of its kind and would perform as advertised: no cracking, peeling, chipping, chalking or color fading for 25 years or we'll come repaint it. It looks great and lasts practically forever. Sure we charge a lot more for it, but if you're interested in maintaining the architectural integrity and exterior appearance of your home for years to come – with no further maintenance on your part – Liquid Siding is the choice for you and I'm the man who can make it happen for you today.

I'm not telling you that belief in what you are representing is critical for some metaphysical reason, but because it is the foundation of everything else you are trying to do. If you are convinced that what you are doing is right for you and beneficial for your customers, then you will persevere in the face of adversity, you will make that extra call every day, ask that tough customer for the sale two or three more times and do whatever it takes to develop your book of business. Without that belief you are more likely to accept objections as legitimate, avoid making calls and feel that any attempt to better yourself or your sales career is just a waste of time.

If you are currently selling and don't believe in the value of your product, I strongly recommend you find a new line to represent. You are holding yourself back and will be amazed at the success you will achieve representing a product you love.

If you are considering a new career in sales, make sure you find a product and a company you can believe in. No product, person or firm is perfect – there are downsides to any proposition – but some are clearly better than others, and one out there is one just right for you. We will discuss this in great detail in *Chapter 5: Choosing The Right Product and Company for You.*

Motivation & Commitment

What's the difference between motivation and commitment? There are a number of ways to look at it.

The wolf is motivated but the rabbit is committed.

Motivation is the back seat of your daddy's car. Commitment is celebrating your twentieth wedding anniversary.

For me motivation is short term, commitment is long term. You might be motivated to try a career in sales, but if you aren't committed to making a success of it you won't last long. The same can be said of virtually any career choice, but the distinction can be drawn much more sharply in sales. The income opportunities can really get people excited (high level of motivation) but the amount of rejection and adjustment to a whole new line of work require a significantly higher amount of ongoing commitment than virtually any other job that doesn't include the potential for bodily injury.

You can learn more about your product and industry, how to be a better listener, organizational skills, how to write sales letters, goal-setting and a whole raft other skills which will help you to be a more successful salesperson. But you can't teach yourself to be committed. And without commitment, mustering the energy every day to learn those other skills will be impossible.

Motivation is an emotional response. Commitment is a personal choice. You can find things that motivate you and use that emotional energy to help maintain your commitment, but you can't rely on that excitement to get you through the tough passages. You must make a personal choice to stick with your new career until you either meet your income goals or a specific period of time has passed. If that period of time isn't at least one year, then you haven't truly made a commitment to a change in career path.

Interpersonal Communications

This is the one area where most people feel they lack what's required to be a "good salesman." I have often heard people say, "I don't have the personality to be a salesperson." To which my response is, "Which personality is that?"

I have known and been called upon by salespeople of every conceivable personality type. I can remember a particular salesman named Dale who used to provide me with printing supplies. Dale was a gentle family man who knew his business inside and out, but he couldn't tell a joke to save his life and never wasted my time with unnecessary banter.

Another salesman named Bill, from a competing firm, was constantly trying to win my business away from Dale. He would bring my staff and me doughnuts, told funny jokes and invited me to baseball games. But he wasn't very good at following up on requests for product information and was a poor listener (we'll talk about the importance of listening in a moment).

Dale on the other hand was a rapt listener who always came through on any commitment he made to me no matter how small. Business decision-makers don't need friends, they need people they can depend on to save them money and help them grow their business. Dale earned all of my business because I knew he always had my best interests at heart. I never could figure out what Bill had at his heart.

Again, based on stereotypes, people assume that a successful salesperson is someone with the gift of gab who could make conversation in almost any situation. Don't get me wrong: that doesn't hurt. But beyond breaking the ice during your first meeting with a new prospect, the ability to run your mouth can cause you more trouble than good.

Still, the fear of stumbling over one's words is enough to keep most people from even considering a career in sales. And, if you never get out of the gate, you'll never cross the finish line. The important point to remember is that it is the fear – not the stumbling – that holds people back.

So if you're one of Brian Tracy's people who "couldn't lead silent prayer in a phone booth" do something about it! Go out and join your local Toastmasters club. There is no better way to work your way through the fear of expressing yourself verbally. (www.toastmasters.org)

Listening

Here's another success factor that you have heard about so often that you're sick of it: Listening Skills. Like those other buzzwords Belief, Motivation and Commitment, you probably figure I'm just trying to get you to buy into something that will build your character. That's not it at all. I encourage you to listen because it will ratchet up your sales production and, if you are not much of a talker to begin with, give you a way to get and keep a dialog going.

Let's face it; in conversation there are only two things you can be doing at any given moment; speaking or listening. There's an old adage that you have two ears and one mouth so you should divide your listening and speaking accordingly. It's human nature to want to speak more than listen and, as a salesperson, you may feel that you have to dominate the conversation in order to inform the prospect of the value of your offering. Nothing could be further from the truth. Prospects like to talk (given the proper prompting) and most people's favorite topic of conversation is themselves.

A great question to open with is, "How can I help you today?" to which the prospect may reply with something like, "Help me? I thought you were here to sell me something!" Your response should be that you don't sell people things, your job is to help people (or printers or homeowners or teachers or car buyers) to make more money (or save more money or sell more printing or provide for the succession of their business or protect their most valuable asset – their home) and that the only way you can do that is by understanding their needs. "So, Mr. Customer, how did you first get into this business (or buy this home or decide you wanted to be a teacher)?" Allow them to take it from there, prompting them only whenever necessary to keep the conversation going.

One important caveat here: you must actually *listen* to what the prospect is saying. If all you are doing is baiting them with questions and then waiting for them to run out of breath so you can begin your pitch, the prospect will feel they are being patronized and you'll be in worse shape than if you had dominated the conversation to begin with. Listen to their words and think about their meaning. Your attention and thought processes will be apparent and appreciated.

You see, sales is not something you do *to* someone, it's something you do *for* someone. By asking intelligent questions and then listening closely to the answers, you allow your customers to sell themselves. They tell you where the pain is and you figure out a way to make it go away. The only way to let them tell you what they want is by listening.

Honesty

Here's another loaded word: Honesty. Again I promote this as a sales skill not because it's morally right but because it's a powerful tool. People are generally guarded when dealing with salespeople. They expect the salesperson to exaggerate, overstate benefits, understate disadvantages, put down the competition and outright lie if necessary. Refusing to fall into that trap can set you completely apart in the mind of the prospect and allow them to drop their guard to really engage with you.

I have had people test me by asking questions that would be easy for me to gloss over, or respond to in a way which would allay their concern – but not be true. Their reaction when I tell them something truthful which they know – on the surface at least – hurts my case, is amazing. People know that no product or service is completely beneficial with no possible downside. But hearing you say it is a revelation.

In fact this approach worked so well that if my prospect didn't ask me one of these tough questions, I'd actually bring up potential disadvantages by saying, "You know, I had a customer ask me one time 'This product has every possible feature you could want. What's wrong with it?' to which I replied 'What's wrong with it? The price of course. This process is expensive!'" I would also talk about certain features which do not meet with every homeowner's needs (such as those preferring a high-gloss finish) which I believe would be sufficient for me to recommend against the installation. The effect on my credibility in the mind of the prospect was often startling.

One more thing about honesty; don't ever be afraid to say, "I don't know" in response to a question. Again, your humanity, humility and honesty will be disarming to the prospect and the potential trouble you could get into by making up an answer will be avoided.

You also never know when someone is asking you a question to which they already know the answer just to test you. If you make up a lie you're busted. But if you tell them you don't know but will find out and get back to them with the answer, you've just given yourself permission to call on them again in the near future.

I seldom found that any single question was sufficiently important to be a deal-breaker anyway, so stressing out over it or dragging out a made-up answer is just a waste of time that gets in the way of a sale.

Regardless of your belief in the efficacy of honesty in the sales environment, I will tell you this: sooner or later lying will catch up with you. And, like they always say, honesty is easier than lying because you don't have to remember which lie you told to whom. In sales, as in the rest of life, honesty really is the best policy.

Acceptance of Varying Lifestyles

Not every person you call upon is going to look like you, live like you, sound like you, worship like you or even smell like you. If you have a hard time accepting people for who they are, you are going to have a tough time in sales.

Again, I promote this not as a moral trait but as a sales booster. The fewer people you are willing to work with the fewer you will sell. Sales is a numbers game, and the top line is the number of people you call upon.

Let's say that, like me, you are a white Anglo-Saxon, middle-aged, heterosexual, Protestant male. But let's also say that, unlike me, you are unwilling to deal with people who aren't like you. What would be the effect on your sales?

Right off the bat you'd lose over 50% of your potential target market if you weren't willing to treat women with respect and do business with them. Carve out all non-whites and you've taken another 50% hit. Exclude Catholics, Jews, homosexuals and people with prominent cowlicks and you're probably down to 10% or less of the total population. Your income potential has thus been seriously jeopardized.

I realize that this is an extreme example, but the fact is that any group that you decide you can't do business with reduces your probability for success. You need every customer you can possibly get your hands on. Bigotry is a luxury you cannot afford.

Some of my best customers at Procraft were gay couples. The people in this group that I have met are generally financially secure, understand the value of quality workmanship, are long-term focused and very concerned about protecting the cosmetic appearance and architectural integrity of their homes – all strong qualifications for having this process done. They are often highly intelligent and widely read. They research their purchase decisions on the Internet and do not part with large sums of money frivolously. From my perspective they were perfect prospects for my business.

Interestingly I had a fellow salesman in this company who was strongly anti-gay. I won't go into the details of his beliefs (which he shared with me more than once) but I will tell you that he felt very strongly. He also thought his feelings did not interfere with his sales work, but the record told a different tale. He never sold a single gay couple (my closing ratio with gay couples was about 80%), and in fact he had one couple call the company to complain about him.

As a salesperson you will meet people of every size and shape, age and personal hygiene level. What you cannot afford to do is prejudge their willingness or ability to buy your product. Salespeople often like to tell stories about the unlikely prospect who ended up being a great customer. Usually those stories involve a person whose first impression was less than impressive. Don't ever let that first impression keep you from making a sale. Ask questions. Get behind the facade to the real person and find out who they are and what makes them tick.

Reading People

This is where sales crosses over a bit into Zen. My wife has a natural ability to read what a person is all about almost immediately and put them at ease. My approach had always been to take people at face value. A successful salesperson cannot afford to do that.

In everyday life, most people put up walls around their true thoughts and emotions. This is particularly true when they are dealing with a salesperson. They believe that the salesperson intends to take advantage of them. They feel vulnerable and become defensive. One of the biggest skills a salesperson can have is the ability to put the person they are meeting with at ease so that their true requirements and desires can be ascertained.

Inasmuch as I was terrible at this initially, I can tell you that this is a skill which can and should be developed. Look around the prospect's home or office. Find out if they are a family man, a sports enthusiast, graduate of a prestigious college, member of a famous organization or family. Get a feel for what they have done in the past, what things are important to them and what decision criteria they might use.

Then focus your presentation and questions in those areas to see whether your initial take on them was correct. You may be dead wrong the first few times. But as you learn and grow, your sense of what motivates individuals will develop over time. This is a skill which can help you in any situation.

Product Knowledge

In the *Introduction* to this book I stressed that product knowledge was not crucial to choosing a sales career in a given industry and even gave an example of an employment ad that supported my assertion. While product knowledge isn't necessary to *starting* a new sales job it certainly is important to *succeeding* at it.

As soon as you land that job you should start asking lots of questions and reading everything you can get your hands on that will increase your knowledge of the industry you have entered and the product or service you are offering. Take advantage of every internal and external educational resource your company offers you. Join local trade groups, attend seminars and role-model after successful salespeople in your company. Maybe someone (either in sales, production or administration) will agree to mentor you.

When I first started at Procraft of Virginia, I didn't know anything about construction, home improvement, carpentry, paint, you name it. And it caused me some embarrassment, particularly when I was presenting to prospects who were knowledgeable about these subjects.

I can remember one gentleman I met early on who told me that he had been a mechanical engineer for 30 years and that it was obvious that I didn't know what I was talking about. Ouch! He told me this after I tried to fudge my way through the answers to a couple of technical questions he had asked me. I should have said, "I don't know but I'll get back to you!" I lost the sale, but I sure learned a valuable lesson.

As I mentioned early on, I tried to do everything I could to learn more about my company, the products we used and the application process we employed. I would continuously come across questions to which I didn't know the answer, but I always made a point of finding the answers – both for my customer and myself. Over time, that approach allows you to build up your own personal database of information you can use to formulate better solutions for your customers' problems. If you don't know how your offering works, how can you possibly use it to help your customers?

Enthusiasm

Here comes another buzzword. I'll keep this one short. If you want your customers to get excited about you, your company and your offering, then you'd better feel the same way first. My sales manager at Procraft, Randy Carter, often referred to the power of emotional transference: whatever you are feeling will be transferred to the emotions of your customer. Enthusiasm is contagious. So is pessimism.

Another sales truism goes something like this: 98% of purchase research is based on logic, but 100% of buying decisions are made emotionally. If you want someone to buy what you're selling, then you need them to become emotionally invested. The best way to do that is by maintaining a high level of enthusiasm yourself.

You don't have to be Polly Perky; in fact I would recommend against that. But you should carry yourself with an air of quiet confidence and subdued excitement if you want your prospects to react positively towards your offering. This way of carrying yourself is also very helpful when responding to objections or picking yourself up after a rejection to make the next call.

Preparation

This is definitely an area you can develop and use to your advantage no matter who you are. The exact definition of that preparation will vary depending upon your offering, your prospect, your experience level and the sales call's position in the sales cycle. But, no matter what, the better prepared you are going in, the better positioned you will be to close the sale.

Let's say you are selling point-of-sale computer systems to restaurant owners. You are about to call on the owner of a small chain of family restaurants. Before you present to him, you would be well served to learn everything you can about his background and the evolution of his food empire.

Sit down for a meal at one or more of his locations. Ask the wait staff and managers questions. What type of sales and cost tracking system is he using now? Does the staff like the current system? What would they like to see improved? How long did he operate a single location before branching out? What type of food does he serve? What does his menu look like? What types of people frequent his restaurants? Does he serve liquor? Who is his competition? Is he looking at your competition? Run Google searches on him and his restaurant. Find out if they have won any awards or been written up in the newspapers.

Find out everything you can before making that call. Then sit down and list all of the ways that your system will benefit him and why he should buy from you instead of your competition. When you meet with him lay out what you've learned and ask him questions which will help you fill in the blanks. Your research and professionalism will impress the prospect. Preparation alone won't close the sale, but it will go a long way to help.

When I was selling Liquid Siding for Procraft, preparation meant making sure my vehicle was ready to go the night before: full of gas, fluids topped off, samples packed, etc. I always kept two calculators, two flashlights, a rolling measuring device, a tape measure, multiple legal pads and ballpoint pens. I even kept felt tips for days when the outdoor temperature was so cold the ballpoints wouldn't write.

I made sure I had plenty of paperwork (contracts, etc.) and my reading glasses. I kept a portable crate-type file holder in the back seat with all of my stuff organized into folders. I even pre-assembled packages of all the paperwork I needed to write up a sale and took them in with me when I presented my price. If you want to close a sale, you need to be prepared to do just that.

Persistence

Another buzzword, right? Maybe so, but it is also a key to sales success. It is self-apparent that as soon as you give up you have failed. If you haven't yet given up you're still in the game. So never give up and never fail.

I didn't make my first sale in this job until my fourteenth presentation, nearly a month into the job. If I had quit after the twelfth presentation I would have failed. I won't tell you that I've never given up on something but I will tell you that I have seen the power of persistence work many times. And some of the most successful people of all time have shown that power at work.

Abraham Lincoln raised himself from poverty and overcame failure in business and politics to become president of the United States. R.H. Macy failed seven times before his store in New York took off. Thomas Edison was expelled from elementary school and tried over 1,000 formulations before perfecting the electric light. Bob Dylan was booed off the stage at a high school talent contest. Mystery writer John Creasey received 753 rejection slips before publishing the first of 562 books.

Bill Porter's mother always exhorted him to keep two words in mind: Patience and Persistence. She would even write those two words in mustard on the bread of the sandwiches she packed him for lunch. Despite Bill's halting speech, his stooped posture, limping gate, deformed hand and shocking appearance, his sheer will to succeed allowed him to persist until he made it happen. How many of us have that same level of fortitude?

We all feel frustration, even despair, when we run into roadblock after roadblock. I'm sure all of the men mentioned above each had many moments of darkness, questioning their abilities, wondering if they were really good enough to make it happen, if the voice telling them to push on was only mocking them. But they persevered and, eventually, succeeded. If, at any point, they had given up, they would have instantly failed.

As a salesperson you will have many rejections and disappointments. Your close ratio (the number of people you sell divided by the total number of people you present to) will most likely resemble a baseball player's batting average. An average of .230 is enough to live on but if you can become a .300 or .400, hitter your paychecks will be knocking your income level out of the park. Nonetheless, even a .400 hitter fails six times out of ten.

Perhaps the most famous story of a salesman whose confidence in his product wouldn't allow him to give up is that of Harlan T. "Colonel" Sanders of Kentucky Fried Chicken fame. At age 63 he turned down an offer of $200,000 cash for the motel-restaurant he had built up over the years. Two years later a superhighway was built that bypassed his business. Twelve months after that he had lost everything.

He could have laid down and died but instead he decided to hit the road. 65 years old and flat broke; he put his recipe and a pressure cooker in his car and traveled the country trying to get restaurants to license his method for cooking chicken. After over 300 rejections, he finally convinced one restaurant owner to pay him 5 cents for every chicken he sold. The rest, as they say, is history.

Never give up and never fail. Give up and fail instantly. Not religion, just fact.

Follow-Up

You may wonder why I list Follow-Up and Persistence separately. To me Persistence means never giving up on your overall goal. Follow-Up means never giving up on an individual prospect or opportunity.

Send the samples you said you were going to send when you said you were going to send them. Call that prospect back in ten days (or tomorrow morning) like you said you would. Return phone messages promptly. Submit price proposals immediately. Do everything with a sense of urgency and a recognition of the value of other people's time.

Follow-Up also means following through. Call back to be sure that the information you sent arrived. This also gives you a chance to ask if there were any questions or anything else you can do to help them arrive at a decision. Check to see how the project you sold is coming along. Call back after it was completed to thank your customer for their business and ask for referrals.

Following up and following through means never having to say you're sorry.

Goal Setting

As a salesperson you are implicitly running your own business. And, as a businessperson, you must set and meet goals if you hope to succeed.

If you are a practiced goal-setter, you will find your transition to sales much easier. If you have avoided the whole concept of setting goals because you didn't want to set yourself up for failure, you may not have the drive required to be a successful salesperson.

There are perhaps hundreds of books on the subject of goal setting, so I won't try to give you a treatise on the subject here. I will only tell you the two things about goal setting that work for me.

First off, set goals that you respond to emotionally. In other words, only set a numerical goal of making, let's say $150,000, if that specific number holds great personal significance to you. Otherwise set goals that involve the acquisition of material objects that you strongly desire (like a second home, cabin cruiser or sports car) or personal achievements (such as beating out last year's top salesman, making the chairman's club or winning a sales contest, college tuition paid in full, two week family vacation in Italy) that really get your blood flowing. Those things that connect with you at a basic level will pull you through tough times. Simply meeting a number will not.

The other important thing about goals is that they must be committed to in writing and brought out and read on a regular basis. Otherwise they are meaningless. If you aren't serious enough about the goal to even put it on paper, how committed can you be to actually making it happen?

Initiative

This is one of those traits that it may be hard to develop if you don't already have it. Not a self-starter? Well get motivated and become one! What's wrong with this picture?

Actually, the one thing that can get a slacker motivated is the right goal. You may have heard the news story a couple of years ago about Japanese mothers who were paying for their sons to have liaisons with prostitutes every time they received an "A" on a test or report card. I am not recommending this approach, but the fact is that these moms knew how to motivate their hormonally-charged teenage offspring. I'll bet that more than a few former class clowns quickly moved to the dean's list.

The financial compensation available in sales may be just the ticket for getting you charged up about your career again. Maybe the reason you're not feeling very motivated right now is because you don't see how you're going to make the kind of money you need to achieve your goals of financial independence, homeownership, college educations for your children, etc.

Any way you look at it, a successful salesperson must show and practice initiative. They have to make the phone calls, do the follow-ups, set the appointments, make the presentations and close the sales. An extension of the old adage that "Nothing happens 'til somebody sells something" could be "If the salesman doesn't do something, we're all out of work!"

With that in mind, one thing which may help you maintain initiative in your sales position is the thought of all of the production and administrative people in your company whose jobs depend upon you. At Procraft there were 8-12 people out every day installing what I had sold. If I didn't sell it, they couldn't get paid for installing it.

Organization

This is a trait that salespeople are notoriously bad at. In many sales jobs there is an ancillary position called Sales Assistant, who does nothing but keep the salesperson on the straight and narrow; maintain his calendar, complete his paperwork, submit reports to management, etc.

These days only the most successful salespeople can expect to get that type of treatment, and the only way to work yourself up to that level is to spend years in the trenches keeping yourself organized. While it is a pain, organization can actually save you a lot of time and make you money. So the sooner you resign yourself to it the better.

We'll talk about using contact management software to keep your calendar and Rolodex organized in a minute. For now let's focus on physical organization. I recommend that you create file folders or job bags for everything. I got into this habit in the printing business: everything related to a live project goes into a single folder; notes, faxes, prices, phone messages, invoices, purchase orders, etc. It may be a mess inside there, but at least you know where everything is. Once the job is completed, everything that needs to be archived is kept in folders identified and sorted by job number or date. Everything else gets thrown away.

Today a lot of the information that is exchanged regarding a given project is in digital form; emails, scans, word processing documents, spreadsheets, etc. I organize everything on my hard drive in folders with customers' names and sub-folders with either job numbers or project names. I also backup my data on a weekly basis because over twenty years of computer operation has proven to me that there are only two types of PC users: those who have had a major hard drive failure and those who are going to have a major hard drive failure.

Consistency

Here's another challenge for high-energy, right-brain oriented salespeople. Doing things the same way every day sounds boring, but it is definitely the path to success in sales. Once you find a system that works, stick with it. Improve it but don't abandon it.

Procraft of Virginia has a long-standing process for performing each call, from the moment you arrive to the moment you leave, and every moment in-between. This process has been honed over many years and has generated many millions of dollars in sales.

When I first started, I liked the scripted approach because I really had no idea what I was doing anyway. Then, as I became more comfortable, I modified the presentation slightly to better fit my delivery, but I never abandoned it or tried to come up with a better system of my own. I believe this is one of the biggest reasons that I reached the level of success that I did.

Drawing on the baseball analogy again, you can look at yourself as a hitter who does the same thing every time he comes to the plate. His coach may make minor adjustments to his swing but, the reason that batter is in the majors is because he knows how to hit the ball. Just keep doing what you do and let the law of averages work for you.

Negotiation

This is a crucial skill for any successful salesperson. I learned a great deal by studying Roger Dawson, a professional speaker specializing in negotiation skills who presented at printing convention I attended in Chicago one year. He gave one helluva presentation and I purchased his $279 "deluxe" package at the back of the room afterwards. There were books, workbooks, audiotapes and videos – all presenting the same skills. But reading, listening and watching the same thing over several times helped me to retain those skills to this day.

I am not going to try to present a thorough treatise on the subject here but I will give you a couple of important points. One is options: whoever has the most alternative courses of action has the most negotiating flexibility. The extent to which you can demonstrate that all of your prospect's alternatives are inferior to what you are presenting will in large part determine your success in closing the deal.

Another very important negotiation tool is perceived willingness to walk away from the deal. If you make it clear by your words and actions that you simply will not accept whatever term or price the prospect has demanded, they must decide how important that particular item really is to them. If, on the other hand, they believe that you are willing to do anything they ask, they may just string you along for days and never end up buying – just to enjoy watching you twist in the wind.

Price is always central to any deal negotiation. While you may not have the power to set pricing you do have the ability to negotiate deals. Price may be the number one stated objective but it is seldom the real thing standing between you and closing a deal. It is crucial to ask questions which will discover the true needs and motivations of the person on the other side of the table.

I have often found it useful to suggest that we, "put price aside for a moment" and talk about all of the rest of facets of the deal. People get very tense when they are considering spending large sums of money so, if you can, take their mind off of that for a while so that you can dig into what's really going on outside of their checkbook.

Never forget that price is not necessarily the same as cost. A customer who is unwilling to spend $30,000 today may be brought to terms with financing – even if their total cost increases by thousands of dollars over the term of the loan.

Be aware of what your company's internal needs are as well. Perhaps there is a surplus inventory of a particular product that they really want to get off the shelves right now. Would your customer be willing to accept a different color or model at a lower price? If so you can make everyone happy including yourself.

Cool Headedness

Many people use emotion as a negotiating tool. They will use emotionally charged words, raise their voice, curse, pound their fist on the table, insult you – try anything they think will cause you to lose your cool and cave to their demands.

As a young man I brought my new car back to the dealership to get a minor problem resolved. I had found that the secondary sun visor (the one you can flip down in front after you have swung the first one to shield the sun coming in the side window) had a rip in its fabric. I hadn't found the problem until I had had the car for a couple of days and wanted it fixed.

Unfortunately the salesman I had dealt with when buying the car no longer worked there. His manager said that he was sorry about the rip but there was nothing he could do about it. I had signed a form which stated that I accepted the car in the condition it was sold to me and the visor was not covered under the warranty. It quickly became apparent to me that the guy was sandbagging me. I got ticked off and told him that I thought his attitude was "bullshit."

His response was that he was insulted and didn't have to stand there and be talked to that way by anyone. He turned his back to me and quickly walked back into the dealership. I was flabbergasted. How could the sales manager of a car dealership possibly be offended by the word I had used? Nonetheless, as a young man with insufficient experience in such things I did not follow him back into the showroom and instead got mad every time I saw that rip over the next four years.

The point is that I had lost my cool. He did not but pretended that he had and used the emotionally charged situation to his advantage. I am not recommending that you follow his model, rather that you not allow others to do it to you. Simply carry on as you had, speaking slowly and calmly, returning to the salient points and working to calm the other person down. If they just won't let go of their tirade, thank them for their time and move on to the next prospect. This is not a sale you're likely to close.

Focus

The word "focus" may sound similar to "consistency" or "organization" or "persistence" but to me it means something a little bit different. Staying focused means not allowing yourself to be distracted by side projects – like writing a book!

Salespeople are generally entrepreneurial, money-motivated and open to new ideas. Because every business needs someone who can sell, opportunities invariably come your way if people believe you are a good salesman.

It can often be difficult to brush these distractions aside, especially if you're beginning to get to a comfort zone in your current job and feel that you could add another lucrative opportunity without hurting your current cash flow.

I won't say, "Don't even consider any other offers" but I will say that the extent to which you let other business opportunities enter your consciousness will directly and negatively impact your ability to make money in your current position.

Contact Management

It is amazing to me how many salespeople don't use contact management software (or don't use it properly) and yet wonder why they haven't achieved more success. Programs like ACT!, GoldMine and even Outlook are designed to combine your address book with your calendar and email to keep you on top of everything you're doing.

Used correctly and consistently they allow you to always keep your promises, return phone calls, arrive at appointments on time, follow-up consistently and close more sales. Unfortunately, many salespeople are too busy to take the time to learn and/or use these tools and end up at the bottom of the sales chart month after month.

If you are serious about a career in sales, you need to make friends with contact management. Find out what other salespeople in your company are using and ask for their help in getting yourself up to speed. Learn how to synchronize the information on your PC with your PDA or cell phone. Create form letters and learn how to do mail merges. Generate fax cover sheets and personalized envelopes. Set alarms to call or follow-up on prospects and clients. Get into the habit and never let it go. You'll be glad you did.

Chapter 4:
The Sales Cycle

Although you may be new to the sales game, you should understand that selling does not occur in a vacuum. Sales is just one part of your company's overall marketing effort.

The period of time which transpires between the initial contact made with a prospect and the actual sale is called the Sales Cycle. Many steps occur during this process and the better acquainted you are with the concept, the more successful you will be in handling your part of the deal.

Sales vs. Marketing

What's the difference between sales and marketing? Well, Stephen Anderson, a sales consultant to the financial planning industry who used to go by the moniker The Cold Call Cowboy, says that marketing is a process and the sale is an event. While I agree with his overall premise, I think that is an oversimplification.

The Five Ps

In business school they tell you that marketing is made up of the five Ps:

1. Product

2. Placement

3. Packaging

4. Price

5. Promotion

Sales is just one part of the fifth P: Promotion. An effective sales presentation requires that all of the other Ps are working in harmony to give the prospect a cohesive picture of the features, functions, benefits and marketplace position of the offering. Similarly, without an effective closing step like direct sales, the other Ps often can't sell the offering on their own.

The idea is that, in order to get people to buy something, you have to look at it holistically. What does our product do for people? Where will we sell it? What sizes, shapes and colors should it be packaged in? How much will people pay for it? And, finally, how are we going to let people know about all of the above?

Climbing back down from the ivory tower to sales in the trenches, it is critical that your company have an overall marketing plan to support your sales efforts. If the features, pricing and packaging of your product have not been well thought-out and tested with buyers, you're going to have a hard time selling it. The same will be true if none of your prospects have ever heard of your company or product before you call on them.

Procraft of Virginia does a great job with marketing. Their advertisements (on radio and television, in newspapers and direct mail) and web site tell the customers enough to understand the features and benefits of the product without stealing the thunder of the salesperson's presentation. This narrows his challenge down to making the presentation and closing the sale, greatly increasing his potential for success.

Prospecting

In most sales positions, your first job is prospecting; finding people for whom your offering is a good match. This involves two steps: qualifying and contacting.

It is very important that you learn the traits that qualify a person to be a great prospect for your offering so you can focus your sales efforts on those most likely to buy. In a consumer-oriented business this would include questions like: How old are they? How much money do they make? Where do they live? What do they do for a living?

In a business-to-business sales position the questions would involve both the company you are targeting as well as the person: What industry are they in? What size is their company? Who are their customers? What are their primary business challenges? Who are their competitors? Where are their offices located? What is typically the title of the person who makes decisions on this type of product within these firms?

Once you have identified your ideal prospect's profile, you must begin attempting to locate and contact those people that best match it. This is the step that most salespeople – even experienced and successful ones – find most distasteful: the networking cocktail parties, the chamber of commerce rubber chicken dinners, asking friends for referrals and so forth.

One of the factors that initially attracted me to Procraft's offering was their provision of a steady stream of pre-qualified prospects. Responding to the company's advertising, homeowners call a toll-free telephone number where operators ask them a series of qualifying questions. If the answers add up, the appointment is made and the lead forwarded to the salesman.

Every day I would receive the name and address of between one and three qualified prospects. My job was to show up on time, make my presentation, measure the property, prepare an estimate, present the price and attempt to close the deal. Not easy, but one helluva lot easier than having to do the prospecting and qualifying too!

As a former business owner I knew the value of these leads and treated them like gold. I never knew what I was going to find when I got there but I always showed up and did the best I could with what I found.

Unless your company has someone else doing the prospecting for you, the task falls to you. There are a number of ways to automate the process and increase your effectiveness over time (and scores of books and seminars on the topic) but there is no escaping it: the first step in the sales process is making contact with the prospect and persuading him or her to agree to a presentation.

Presenting

This is perhaps the most crucial step. Being as you never get a second chance to make a first impression, it is critically important that you are fully prepared prior to every presentation. Every salesperson's goal is to close the sale in the first presentation, but in many cases this is unrealistic. With that in mind you need to create a realistic objective going into the meeting and make sure you come out with that objective met.

Without going over territory we have already covered, I would highly recommend that you do more listening than speaking – particularly at the beginning of the presentation. Get the prospect talking by asking them questions about themselves. Whenever possible ask questions that relate – at least tangentially – to your offering and their needs which relate to it. When the time feels right, transition into your presentation as nimbly as possible.

As you present, try to remain as conversational as possible. Maintain eye contact. Vary the speed and pitch of your speech. Use natural hand gestures. Lean forward to emphasize certain points and lean back to an upright position once the point is made. Stop when the prospect indicates, either verbally or visually, that they have a question. Don't answer the question before the prospect has finished asking it – even if you've heard the exact same question one thousand times before. Consider your answer before responding, and then try to provide the answer thoughtfully, not robotically.

Every presentation should have a forecasting statement telling the prospect what to expect and how much of their time you need. If they are interested, you can take as much time as you need. If they aren't, more time isn't going to help you. You should have three areas to cover. Let them know when you're moving from a completed point to a new one.

When you're finished, it shouldn't be a mystery. "That's our story" is a way I would often finish a presentation. "Do you have any questions?"

Closing

If they don't have questions, ask for the sale. Act as though their lack of questions implies that they are ready to buy. "So may I take your order?"

This is what's called The Close. Depending upon where you are in the presentation it could be The Trial Close, The Doorknob Close or somewhere in-between. Some salespeople say that you should Always Be Closing (the ABCs of sales), but I don't agree. I only begin to close when the time is right – although that time differs from one presentation to the next.

One thing I always do throughout the presentation is look for buying signals. Certain questions that people ask indicate that they are serious about your offering. Looks between husbands and wives can be very telling. And even something as straightforward as the prospect picking up a pen or getting out their checkbook should not be ignored.

Another truism in sales is once the person says "yes," you should shut up. Failure to do so is known as talking through the sale or talking your way out of a sale. It sounds crazy but you would be surprised how often this can happen to salespeople who are accustomed to getting a lot of nos from prospects. They make their presentations so methodically and are so accustomed to being turned down, that they don't pick up on the fact that they have the person sold – even when the prospect comes right out and says, "Enough already, I'm sold."

Overcoming Objections

But what if they really are saying no? In sales lingo a prospect who says "no" is simply giving you an objection. Your job as a salesperson is to overcome objections. Again, many volumes have been written on the fine art of overcoming objections. I will give you just a couple of tips from my experience.

At Procraft, where the one-call close is almost a religion, I found that many people who really were ready to buy would give me objections just because they wouldn't feel right rolling over and saying yes without a bit of a fight. Others were ready to buy but were just looking for some small concession – price or otherwise – in order to feel like they were doing the right thing.

The most important thing about overcoming objections is listening closely to how the prospect describes their discomfort. They are saying the price is too high but is it that they can't afford it or that they just don't think the benefits are equal to the cost? Is it a cash flow issue where the price would be more acceptable if it were broken up into multiple payments? Is there a number they are thinking of that they can see their way clear to agreeing to? Again, listening and asking questions are key to success in overcoming objections.

The Sound of Silence

Another very important tool is silence. Most people – salespeople included – cannot bear silence in a conversation. Tolerating silence across a table is a skill you need to develop. Once you have tossed the monkey into your prospect's lap – whether it be a price proposal or other suggested course of action – you need to shut your mouth and let them tell you what's going to happen next. Don't assume for a moment that you know what they are going to say and don't let them off the hook by saying something yourself.

At Procraft I found that the ten seconds after I presented the price (and then shut-up) were the most important of my entire visit. The next words said would tell me almost instantly whether or not I had a shot of closing the deal.

After several seconds of uncomfortable silence, the best thing I could hear was, *"Well honey, what do you think?"*

I remained silent.

"It sure seems like a lot of money Bob."

Still I remained silent.

"Yeah, but I sure don't want to get up on that ladder anymore and we haven't been able to find a reliable painter in years."

He was overcoming her objections for me.

I continued to remain silent.

"Alright honey. Whatever you want is okay with me."

Bingo!

Naturally, they didn't all go that way. Sometimes the first thing I would hear is "Thank you very much for coming to tell us about this, but that's a lot more than we want to spend." At which point I would begin asking questions to find out what they did want to spend, how far off I was and how we might still come to a common resolution.

No matter what the outcome though, having the strength to keep your mouth shut at the right time is a skill every salesperson should learn.

Follow-Up In Action

Maybe you're not in a one-call close kind of business. Or maybe you just didn't close during your first, or most recent, call. Now what? Follow-up, that's what.

The question here is how can you be persistent at following up without making a nuisance of yourself? The answer is light, consistent touches. Using your contact management software or any number of automated online systems, you can send personalized letters, postcards, color emails or other communications to your prospect on a pre-set schedule. These light touches should be interspersed with telephone calls and the occasional unannounced visit.

Every prospect is different, and no two situations are identical, but my choice is to err on the side of being a little annoying. Let's face it, people expect salespeople to be assertive. Most businesspeople even appreciate it, and know your livelihood depends upon it. If I am aware of a prospect for whom my offering represents a huge value, I will keep touching until they either buy, die or tell me explicitly to go away. For some salespeople this "dripping" process can literally go on for years before resulting in a sale.

Referrals and Repeat Business

I would be remiss in closing this chapter without spending a moment to talk about repeat and referral business. Considering all of the effort that is put into prospecting, presenting to and closing customers, why in the world would you ignore the potential to generate additional business from people who have already purchased from you?

There are those who say that if you don't have 100% of your customers' budget for your offering, your current client list is your most fertile hunting ground. Make sure that all of your clients know everything you do. Find out why they aren't placing all of their business with you and keep dripping on them until they say yes.

Referral business is another area where many salespeople overlook one of their best opportunities. This is generally because they don't have a systematic approach to the problem. It is estimated that 20% of a given salesperson's clients would willingly provide him or her with referrals to friends and associates simply by being asked. Another 20% wouldn't provide a reference for Moses. The remaining 60% will most probably offer references if they are only shown how.

There are scores of resources available on the subject of generating referrals. Every salesperson should actively ask for referrals and should have a system in place that makes it easy for their customers to give up the names and contact information. Do whatever you can to demonstrate how you will communicate with the third party (show a copy of the form letter of introduction for example) and assure your client that you will not make a nuisance of yourself. If possible, ask them to call the third party right there and then and put you on the phone.

For a great, systematic approach to building your business through referrals, check out John Jantsch's **Referral Flood** *at http;//www.ReferralFlood.com or call John at 816-561-3931.*

Chapter 5:
Choosing The Right Product and Company for You

Well, if you've made it this far into the book, you must be seriously considering making the move to a career in sales. The big question left in your mind is probably, "What should I sell?"

The answer to that question depends upon a number of variables, including:

1. How much money do you want to make?

2. How much risk are you willing to tolerate?

3. How much travel can you and your family cope with?

4. How much money do you have in the bank?

5. What are your current skills, passions and connections?

I like to start with the money question because numbers are quantifiable and, by driving a stake in the ground here, you can begin to develop your overall plan around that income target. Unfortunately, even money has its own sub-variables such as timeframe and downside risk vs. upside potential.

For example, let's say your goal is to make $150,000 in your second or – at worst – third year at your new sales job. Again, that's the second or third year, not five years out. Anyone whose income last year was in five figures and wishes to move to $150,000 in the next year or two must come to some harsh realizations:

1. You are going to have to work your butt off

2. It is unlikely that there will be any base salary involved

3. You may have to travel extensively

For your first year in sales with a new company in a new industry this goal would probably be unrealistic. But, depending on the company and offering you connect with, it could be entirely doable in the very near future.

Right now however, we're talking about what you want to make, not how you're going to make it.

Money and Risk

Let's assume for the moment that you are not afraid of hard work and recognize that it comes with making great money. We can also assume that, if you find something you really like and see it paying off, the time you spend on the job will not seem so much like work.

That brings us to item 2: no base salary. If you can find a sales job – or any job for that matter – that has a $150,000 in second- or third-year income potential which includes a living salary baseline, you should be the one writing this book. The fact is that most sales jobs that have unlimited upside potential offer little or no safety net.

It's just part of the risk-reward calculation. Management puts both the risk and the reward on you as a carrot-and-stick motivational program. If you aren't hungry, the theory goes, you aren't sufficiently motivated to go out there and make some rain. Comfort breeds complacency, and complacency is a bad trait in a salesperson.

Until I started selling Liquid Siding I couldn't really grasp this concept – from either side of the table. When trying to get the dot-com company going I hired five or six salespeople and a Vice President of Sales, all of whom were supposed to bring clients with them and begin building a new book of business with us. I made the mistake of putting them all on salary which was supposed to ratchet down over time to give them income during the transitionary period as they built up their commissions on new work. Only one of those people ever generated any significant sales volume. The rest picked up their checks and delivered only excuses.

At the time I couldn't see how we could attract successful salespeople without offering them some level of guaranteed income. In retrospect I realize the reason for that was that the opportunity we were presenting was too risky. People who had successful sales careers with established companies were not willing to put all of that at risk to move to a new company with an unproven business model without some type of guaranteed income. We didn't have a proposition that was attractive to real salespeople.

There are any number of sales jobs which fit this model of unlimited upside potential with no safety net. Many of them you are very familiar with: Realtor, insurance agent, auto salesman and so forth. Most of the people who have found success in these industries have built a book of business over time, not overnight.

Your Current Bank Account

This is where the amount of money you have in the bank comes in. If you can't support yourself through the ramp-up period, you probably shouldn't consider a commission-only job. There's an old saying in sales that goes, "If you really need a sale you'll never get it." Prospects can smell your desperation and will avoid doing business with you at all costs.

Let's swing to the other side of the spectrum and consider a sales job that offers only a salary, such as in many retail environments like big box stores and jewelers. Here you will find a work environment much like an office from the standpoint of it being a single building to which you commute daily.

You will sell a relatively static set of products to people who come to you (pre-qualified buyers requiring no prospecting). You will be paid an hourly wage or weekly salary along with performance bonuses (in some cases) and, if you're lucky, a benefits package. The downside of course is that you probably will have a ceiling on your earning potential.

There are a number of jobs which fall somewhere in-between, offering a base salary and benefits – at least for some period of time – with varying levels of upside potential. Some, in the IT services and software industries for example, have hefty base pay of as much as $75,000 and potential total compensation levels of $250,000 or more, but they are very particular about whom they hire. If you don't have a strong level of product knowledge, technical expertise and/or an existing book of business to bring over, you probably don't have a chance of landing one of these jobs.

In other cases you will find what is called a draw against commissions, also known as a recoverable draw. Here the company will pay you a fixed amount every pay period even before you make your first sale, but you are responsible for paying back those draws out of future commissions earned. The sooner you start generating sales, the less of an issue this will be. If you go a number of months without any production, you will go deep in the hole and the company will probably let you go – at which point the draw is no longer recoverable (in most cases).

Obviously there is a wide range of commission structures out there. What you need to do is consider your income goals within a time frame and determine where you want to be money-wise in one, three, five and ten years. Then consider which type of commission structure best matches your current financial situation and your level of risk aversion.

You may find that it would be best for you to assume less risk at first as you learn the sales trade and build up your bank account and then switch to a more lucrative – and riskier – position later, when you are more secure in both your skills and your finances.

Travel

Some of the most lucrative sales positions require extensive travel. Again, this is an element that many people can't or won't tolerate which prevents them from considering sales as a career.

At Procraft all of my travels were by car, and none required even an overnight stay, much less several days away from home. However, I did drive hundreds of miles per week, sometimes as many as 200 miles in a single day. Luckily I enjoy driving and most of my travels were during non-rush times. I often drove on beautiful country roads and got to see little towns and hamlets that most people will never experience.

I probably would not take a job that required extensive air travel. This preference limits my options and potentially my income. You will have to decide what works best for you. I know one person, not a salesperson, whose willingness to fly all over the world at a moment's notice has, in part, been responsible for their ability to amass a multi-million dollar personal net worth.

If my experience is any guide, you can find a number of high-paying sales jobs that do not require overnight travel. But the very nature of the position requires that you meet with a high volume of people on an ongoing basis. If they are not coming to you (a la a retail store), you must go to them. One way or another you will be on the move.

The Offering

So, we have examined some very important decision criteria, but we really haven't gotten to the root issue of what to sell and who to work for. That's because, until you have considered what your personal motivations and requirements are, you aren't in a position to think about the company you want to work for or the offering you want to present.

I believe that, after considering the financial, risk and travel variables presented above, you should decide upon the offering first and then find the best company to work for. Deciding upon the offering can be difficult if you let it, but don't forget my experience: I had absolutely no idea what I was getting into and still found that I loved the offering and the job and, after a fitful start, was successful at it.

Analysis is great, but don't let it lead to paralysis. I once read that the only thing more important than making the right decision was making any decision. Even the wrong decision can be made right with hard work. But the avoidance of a decision can never be made right. Sooner or later you need to go for it with an attitude of commitment to see it through no matter what.

> *A quick side note: You may choose to sell an offering which is either a product or a service. In order to avoid the repetitious use of the phrase "product or service" I will usually refer either to "offering" or "product."*

The perfect offering would involve a product or service that you are passionate about, are expert at and can make a ton of money selling. For a car guy this could mean automobile retailing. For a computer dweeb it could be selling software, web hosting services, IT consulting or network management. Not that many people are passionate about insurance, but many are regarding real estate, architecture, art, diamonds, clothing, event production, catering, web development or construction. You might want to break into the broadcasting industry and see radio advertising sales as your foot in the door.

Just about anything you can think of has a lucrative sales position somewhere in the food chain. The trick is to find the right point. The bigger the dollar value of an individual transaction, the better chance there is to find a fat commission. But lower-priced items can be lucrative to sell as well – as long as you're moving a lot of volume and look for your spot further up the chain.

Let's say you're a fanatic about mountain biking. I would imagine there is some amount of money to be made in selling $2,500 bicycles and accessories at a retail store – depending upon how many you're able to move every week. A more lucrative spot might be working for the distributor that supplies those shops or even an event company that produces competitive rides.

What if you love entertaining? You could do sales for a catering company, a wedding planner or event production company. You might also choose to work in sales at the catering department of a large hotel or meetings facility. You could also sell for any number or companies that provide supplies, services and/or logistical support to the hospitality industry.

Staying Close To Home

One natural choice would be to pursue a sales position in the industry you're currently working in. You have the product knowledge. You know how the business works. You know who the most lucrative clients are, and you've seen the salesmen who work for your company make a lot of money. Sounds perfect, right?

Well, it can be, depending upon a couple of factors. The first is whether you really want to stay in your current industry. Your search for a sales position may also be an indication that you're looking for something completely new. Have a little talk with yourself on that subject and see what you have to say. You might be surprised.

The other thing I would recommend against is applying for a sales job within your current company. There are plenty of reasons this might sound good: familiarity, seniority, etc. But your co-workers may not be as willing to accept your new sales veneer as you are. And, if you fail, it may be next to impossible to get your old job back.

A famous person once said, "A prophet is not without honor save in his own home." My take on that one is that people have a hard time seeing someone they know in a new light, whether it be Jesus returning to Nazareth or you showing up with a suit and briefcase when you normally wear golf shirts and boat shoes. If you want everyone, including you, to buy into your new identity as a salesperson, I suggest you start fresh someplace new.

If All Else Fails

If you still don't have any idea what offering you'd like to represent, perform the following exercise. Keep a small reporter's notepad (like the kind detectives write in on TV cop shows) with you and every time something strikes you as funny, interesting, exciting or in any way emotionally appealing, write it down. Whatever tastes good, sounds good, feels good, looks good or smells good, write it down. Anything that makes you laugh, ask a question or put your hand to your mouth and say "hmm," write it down.

Over the course of a month or so you will begin to see a pattern of the things that really interest you in this life. It could involve children, sports, the Internet, your house of worship, architecture – who knows? As you begin to see those areas come into focus, begin to ask yourself what types of sales jobs might be associated with them.

Believe it or not, law firms and architects need sales and marketing. Most churches are looking for ways to increase the size of their congregations. Youth clubs, associations, charitable organizations – all kinds of groups that you may never have considered before – are all looking for people who can bring in dollars.

The Company

After finding two or three very appealing offerings, you are now ready to take the final step of choosing the company(s) you want to work for.

No two companies are alike – or even similar! Every company has their own way of doing things, their own corporate history and culture. From the perspective of a potential salesperson, the four things you want to look for in a prospective employer, in no particular order, are:

1. Marketing and Sales Support

2. Administrative Systems

3. Production Expertise

4. Financial Security

In general, companies with a longer track record are going to score higher on all four of these items. They know how to market and they aren't afraid to expend resources on advertising. They probably have long-standing marketing and sales systems in place which have been successfully pumping out qualified prospects for years.

An older company may not, however, have the best administrative systems. Their paperwork flow may be archaic and redundant. 21st Century concepts like email and electronic forms submission could be out of the question. All of the paperwork falls to the salesperson, and nobody gets paid until everything is submitted – correctly – in triplicate.

Marketing vs. Production

Newer firms, on the other hand, may have the latest in wireless order entry and submission, but their production and delivery may not have caught up yet. Sometimes successful marketing organizations look upon actually delivering the goods to the customer as a necessary evil.

If production appears to be an afterthought at a company you are considering, you might want to think twice before joining up. Salespeople make the promises but everyone else make the trains run on time. Customers don't forget the promises they were told or who told them. You don't want to have to be continuously answering to your customers for other people's shortcomings.

I'll give you a couple of examples. Back in my printing days I competed against a huge local company that was one of the largest commercial printers in the entire country. They had all the latest equipment, multiple locations, hundreds of employees and tens of millions of dollars in sales. I hated those guys. No, really.

Every time I bid against them they won. I tried everything I could think of to position myself as more nimble, more customer focused, better able to deliver personalized services, etc., but it never worked. These guys had a huge sales force of well-trained and handsomely compensated closers. I wasn't a salesman. I didn't stand a chance.

Years later (after we had sold our print shop) a close friend of mine went to work for this company. Her perspective from the inside shocked me. The production floor was an utter disaster. Scores of jobs were being produced incorrectly or delivered late. Each department jealously guarded their territory and refused to communicate with other parts of the plant. The management approach seemed to be, "The beatings will continue until morale improves."

It turned out that the founder of the company had semi-retired and the production guy who had been his number two was passed over when it came time to name a successor. The production guy moved on to another company and the sales guy, who got the top job, maintained his focus on what he knew. In a very short period of time this 35 year-old company began losing huge chunks of business, closing locations and bleeding red ink. All the marketing and sales prowess in the world couldn't put Humpty Dumpty back together again. And many of the highly-trained sharks started looking for smoother waters.

The same thing happened to Xerox in the late 1990s. Here was a company with a world-renowned sales culture getting their butts kicked in the marketplace, at the stock market, in the halls of academia and at the SEC. All their sales know-how couldn't help when their machines broke down due to poor design and their service techs didn't know how to fix them because the technical literature and training wasn't being distributed properly. A new CEO came in, cleaned house and got the company back on track. I look for them to regain their place as one of America's premier firms in the next few years.

The moral? Don't underestimate the importance of your company's ability to deliver on your promises as an income driver for you, the salesperson. And don't be swayed by a glitzy sales culture, fancy collateral material and an unbelievable compensation plan unless you know the rest of the company is just as strong.

Financial Strength

Speaking of strength, one of the most important advantages a prospective employer in the sales game can have is financial soundness. Here again, older companies generally have the advantage. Unless a newer company was founded by someone with deep pockets, has significant venture capital backing, or otherwise is flush with cash, it may have a hard time managing its cash flow sufficient to pay those big commission checks.

This is not to say that all newer companies are illegitimate, only that a successful sales push may outrun the bank account's headlights, leading to periods of anxiety early on. Depending upon the company's cost structure and customer payment terms, this may not necessarily be the case. But when investigating and interviewing, I would strongly suggest that you find out all you can about the financial security of the company you are considering hitching your wagon to.

You can politely mention this during the interview by saying something like "One thing I really like about your company is its financial stability." If the person on the other side of the desk flinches, blushes, chokes or – worst of all – busts out laughing, you may have hit a hot button. You may also want to purchase information on a prospective employer via an online service such as Hoovers, Dun and Bradstreet or USSearch.com.

The only way to be able to compare and contrast prospective employers based upon the criteria listed above is to go on a large number of interviews and do your homework. Hoping and wishing that a company is going to be a strong match for your personal criteria isn't going to make it so. This is your career, your life. Don't be afraid to do some work to make sure that the company you are going to be depending upon for your livelihood – and to back up the promises you are going to be making to customers – is worthy of that trust.

Chapter 6:
Selling Yourself

Following the guidelines in the previous chapter, you've identified one or more offerings and companies that you'd like to represent as a salesperson. You're interested in the product, are comfortable with the risk/return ratio and income potential, feel good about the companies you are targeting and are now ready to start selling yourself to them as the person who can make it happen. This is where the rubber really meets the road.

From a sales perspective, your work to this point has been to identify and qualify prospects for your offering. Now is the time for the sales cycle to start. Just like a salesperson, you are going to have to jump through some hoops to secure interviews and then do some selling when you finally get in front of a few prospective customers. Refer back to *Chapter 3: The Sales Skill Set*, do your homework up front, listen closely and ask for the sale.

The Interviewer's Perspective

In my previous lives as a business owner and manager I have reviewed hundreds of resumes and conducted scores of employment interviews. As a result I have experience on both sides of the table; both as interviewer and as interviewee. Neither side is a heck of a lot of fun. Since the employment interviewer is a customer I understand, let me give you a little insight into his thinking.

You're not the only one who is frustrated, burned-out and sometimes nervous about the interviewing process. Choosing a person to fill a job is one of the most difficult things a manager has to do. I have hired many people I thought were going to be fantastic – perfect for the position – who ended up being unreliable, terrible with customers, living out of their car, battling alcoholism, you name it. Only once did I hire someone for a hard-to-fill position who I thought was going to be only marginally effective that turned out to be unbelievably organized, loyal and productive. The bottom line is that it's hard to find good help these days - and it always has been.

The new employee's effectiveness is reflected upon the person who hired them – whether for good or ill. Managers try hard to weed out the bad players and find the best possible candidate. Unfortunately most managers have many other priorities in their day and could wish that the whole hiring process would go away.

And hiring people is a process. It begins with writing a job description that includes responsibilities, performance evaluation factors and timetable, salary and benefits, who that position reports to and who reports to that position. All of these questions should have been answered by management at the beginning of the process. If not, they can expect the employee to be asking before long.

The next step is advertising the position. If you have never written a help wanted ad, you have no idea how difficult this can be. Your ad will be competing with scores of others seeking that elusive person: someone who is smart, sober, reliable, organized, presentable and able to sell. At the same time you have a limited number of words you can use to communicate the value and opportunity that the job represents. You have to decide which sections to place the ad in, what headline to use, whether to give a phone number, fax number, email or web site address for responses, etc.

Many ads are placed without sufficient consideration being given to these matters. The results are amateurish and the pulling power of the ads limited. Too often classified ads are written from the perspective of management rather than from that of the optimum candidate. Savvy employers place ads that speak directly to the people they hope to attract. In the case of top-producing salespeople, that means references to earning potential, frequency of payout, pre-qualified prospects, corporate stability, financial strength, advancement based on merit, etc.

It's widely known that the best day to run newspaper employment ads is Sunday. On Monday the fun begins: people start responding. Like a police department asking for the public's help in solving a crime, employers can expect to hear from every crank in town when they place an ad.

Plowing through the resumes and finding three to five people you want to spend time interviewing can be a daunting task. But it's critical not to waste time meeting with people who aren't even in the running. Smart employers will separate out the non-contending resumes, do pre-interviews over the telephone with the contenders and then schedule face-to-face interviews with the hot prospects.

Spending even an hour interviewing each of five candidates can be exhausting. And yet, can you really make an informed decision about such a complicated task as plugging a human being into a job with only 60 minutes of interaction? Probably not, but that's the way it often goes.

As a safeguard, most companies will put new employees on a 90-day probation period during which time they receive no benefits, are not classified as full-time workers and can be fired at any time without cause. Just as you never really know someone until you live with them, there is no way to know how someone will perform in a job until you see them in action for a period of time.

The Interviewee's Perspective

Let's swing back to your side of the table now. If you want to make it through the gauntlet described above, get your story in front of the right person, make it to the interview stage and be selected for the job, you're going to have to work at it!

Everything you do should be directed towards communicating to the relevant decision-maker that you are the person who will make them look brilliant for having hired you. Pay attention to the requirements listed in the ad and position yourself as a strong match in every communication you have with them, from cover letter and resume through telephone and personal interviews. Don't gild the lily too much by exaggerating how your experience exactly fits their needs or even lying to cover any holes in your resume. But never stop stressing how well you know you can do the job and how your hiring will benefit the firm.

Your Sales-Focused Resume

It is not a sin to have more than one resume. If you are applying for multiple types of jobs, you need multiple resumes.

But how do you position yourself for a sales job if your resume doesn't show any sales experience? The answer is to stress things that you have done which are success factors in a sales environment. For example, anything you have done which involves interaction with customers:

customer service representative; field claims representative for an insurance company; telephone operator taking inbound calls; greeter at Wal-mart; receptionist, etc.

Anything you have done which is communications-oriented is also good: public speaking (are you a member of Toastmasters?); any writing credits you can offer – from the church newsletter to a trade magazine. The basic point here is to make it clear that you know how to communicate a concept to an uninitiated recipient.

Working under stress and meeting deadlines is very important in sales as is the setting and meeting of goals. Any experience you can point to which demonstrates your abilities in these areas will be helpful.

Remember the ad I quoted in the *Introduction* to this book. That computer company was looking for the right person; someone with drive and energy. "We can teach the rest." You don't have to lie about what you can do. If people get the impression that lying is your strongest skill, they aren't likely to hire you.

You can also position your lack of sales and product-specific experience as an advantage. You are green, ready to be developed and molded in the company's image of the perfect representative. You don't have any preconceived notions about how things are supposed to be done that have to be "trained out of you."

You are ready to learn everything they have to teach you and do things exactly as they direct you. Experienced salespeople with successful track records are often more confident in their own methods and less willing to do things the "company way." Sales managers know this and have dealt with recalcitrant hot shots in the past. Your greenness is a benefit to them – especially if they hear you say so.

Processing The Classified Ads

No doubt about it: looking for a job is a pain. But, if you're serious about it, you need to approach it systematically to give yourself the highest probability of succeeding.

My system begins with making a two-hour appointment with yourself every Sunday to review and respond to ads in the newspaper. Find a quiet spot in your home that contains a flat horizontal surface (desktop, card table, etc.) and a trashcan. Put everyone on notice that you are not to be disturbed until further notice. Then take the newspaper, a fresh spiral notebook, scissors, transparent tape, a couple of ballpoint pens – one red and one black – and a stapler in there and don't come out until you are finished with the steps below.

First you are going to find and mark any and all jobs of interest to you. There should be at least two category headings of interest to you: Sales and whatever industry(s) you are targeting. Sometimes employers will put their ads for salespeople within their industry category rather than, or in addition to, the Sales category. You will, for example, often find ads for printing sales positions listed both under Printing and Sales. Determine which category headings you are interested in ahead of time and confine your search there to maximize the effective use of your time.

As you browse the paper, use the red ballpoint pen to draw diagonal lines at the corners of each ad that you want to cut out. Don't be terribly discriminatory at this point. Mark every ad that you may have any interest in; we'll weed out the less attractive ones in a moment. Go from the beginning to the end of your sections without stopping. If you do stop, you'll have one heck of a time figuring out where you left off.

Next, re-read the ads you have marked and use your scissors to cut out the ones that you still feel strongly enough about to put your full energy into applying for. If the job sounds only marginally appealing you're probably not going to be willing to do everything I describe below in an attempt to win it for yourself.

You should limit your selections to 10-12 ads to respond to each week. Anything more and you're going to burn out quickly, finding it hard to muster the energy to go back into that room next Sunday. Anything less and you're not really giving this your best shot. Just like sales, job-hunting is often a numbers game. The higher number of jobs you apply for (within reason) the higher your probability of finding the one that's right for you.

Be sure to use your scissors. Don't tear or rip the ad out because you are likely to tear right through it. As an old printer I can tell you that the paper will tear cleanly with the grain (usually up and down on the sheet) but not against the grain. Rip at your own risk.

Now tape each of the 10-12 ads in the upper right-hand corner of individual sheets of ruled paper in your spiral notebook. On each sheet write the date and newspaper the ad came from, along with the heading it was listed under.

For each ad chosen, see if you can find a web site on that company or any other information available online such as newspaper articles or customer complaints on message boards. Find out how long they have been in business, how many locations they have, their size (in revenue and number of employees), what companies they partner with, their ownership, management, customer list – anything that can help you decide if they and their offering meet your personal criteria. All of this information will also be valuable in preparing your responses and, potentially, during the interview process.

Write down anything relevant on the page you have taped the ad to. If there is too much information to list, write down the URLs (web addresses) where you found the info and leave yourself a note regarding your overall impression of the firm: favorable or negative. These notes will be critical later when you receive replies from companies wishing to move forward with you. You may even choose to eliminate some prospective employers at this point if you find information about them that really turns you off or doesn't match your personal priorities.

Responding to Ads

There are three primary ways that employers ask to receive resumes: 1) via fax; 2) as an attachment to an email message; 3) posted to their web site. You need to be ready for any and all of the above.

Your resume should be in Microsoft Word format. If you don't have a computer or don't have Word, you will have to hire someone to create the resume for you and find a way to modify it yourself – perhaps at the local Kinko's. There's no way around it: without a computer, Internet access and Microsoft Word, you will be at a significant competitive disadvantage in the jobs marketplace. If you've got a lot of time to invest you can work around it, but the remainder of this chapter assumes that you do have those tools available.

I started by taking my existing resume and molding it to better address sales openings. While I had never worked as a salesperson, I talked about how much sales grew at the print shop under my leadership. I positioned the capital raising I did at the dot-com company as sales work (not much of a stretch really). I highlighted my experience as a public speaker and my marketing communication experience.

I had intended to send the same resume to every sales ad but found that that just didn't work. While I may be at the extreme end of the spectrum, I ended up editing my resume for just about every job I applied for. I also saved a separate copy of each resume in a folder called "Resumes" on my hard drive. Each one was named

Felker_Resume_Company.doc, where "_Company" was the name of the company I was sending the resume to. If I heard back from a given company, I could then review the resume I had sent them and compare it with the requirements listed in their original ad.

The naming of this document is not trivial. If you are emailing it, the recipient will see the document name and may save a copy on their hard drive as well. They may search for your resume later by your name, so be sure to include it. Don't use any silly abbreviations or accidentally send Jones & Co. a resume saved as Smith & Co. And don't call your resume Felker_Resume_Sales_03.doc. This will tell them that you are applying for jobs both within and without the sales field and that you definitely have multiple resume versions floating around.

Posting Your Resume To A Web Site

If the ad asks you to fax or email your resume, you can move on to my suggestions below. But, if the ad asks you to post your resume to a web site, you have a new challenge ahead of you. Most of these web-based resume receptacles accept only text pasted into their allotted fields, not Microsoft Word files. This sounds simple enough: just copy the text from your resume and paste it into the intended spot on the web page. The problem is that you lose all typestyle – no bold or italics – everything is flush left and some of your carriage returns will disappear. Be sure to proofread what you have pasted before clicking on the button that sends the text to their server.

There are also often limits to the number of characters you can post, which means that you may need to delete some words, paragraphs or even entire sections or pages from your resume in order to make it fit. You also will not have the opportunity to print out and proofread this truncated version, nor will you have a copy of it to refer to when and if the company contacts you or asks you to come in for an interview.

Requests to post your resume to a web site are generally a bad sign. Rather than being read by human beings, these posted resumes are generally searched by computer programs looking for key words that management thinks fit their requirements. This is also an indication that you are dealing with a larger, more impersonal company that is processing huge numbers of resumes being posted by your competitors.

Responding Via Fax or Email

Sending your resume by fax is the closest thing to the antiquated notion of mailing it to a prospective employer with a cover letter attached. There are some important distinctions however. There is no envelope used, no postage attached and no possibility of having your resume lost in the mail. The employer receives your information almost instantaneously and you have confirmation of that fact.

Every resume you send by email, fax or USPS must include a cover letter, addressed from you to the recipient named in the ad – even if that recipient is "Box 182-RE." The letter should be in standard business format with the date and recipient information at the top and your contact information including phone number below the signature block at the bottom.

If the recipient is anonymous the salutation line should read "To whom it may concern," If a name is given and you are sure of the recipient's sex, use "Dear Ms. Jones," or "Dear Mr. Smith" not their first name. Your closing above the signature block should say either "Sincerely," or "Regards,"

I include the cover letter as the first page of the resume Word document. This is part of the personalization of each resume. It makes it easier to keep everything from each of my responses in one document and it means that there is only one attachment to the emails I send. Both of these factors are important because the cover letter often imparts information in a way that a resume cannot.

In your cover letter you can be more conversational than the generally staid language used in a resume. You can speak directly to the requirements listed in the ad, talk about how well your experience matches up with them and impart a bit of your own personality into the communication. This can be taken too far, but I would recommend that you open the letter by thanking the recipient for taking the time to review your resume, continue with information relative to how your qualifications match their needs, and close with an indication that you look forward to meeting with them to discuss the opportunity further.

Whether emailing or faxing your resume, you should include a pseudo-signature in a script font or bold-italic version of a serif font in the middle of the signature block. If your resume looks like solid gold but your signature looks like axe murderer, you probably won't get called in for an interview. Guess what my signature looks like.

When emailing a resume, your email message is essentially a second cover letter. My approach is to keep the email message exceedingly short and let the cover letter speak for itself. My email messages thank the recipient for accepting my resume and reference what position I am applying for. I also include the position title in the subject line.

After transmitting my resume and cover letter I write down in the spiral notebook how and when I responded to the ad. As I receive calls or email responses from prospective employers, I note those on the appropriate pages in the notebook as well. Over time you begin to see a picture appearing of what is working for you and what is not. This allows you to perfect your approach and gives you an even better chance of landing exactly the job you want.

Searching The Online Job Sites

Despite what they say in their television ads, these sites do not work automatically. You can't just post your resume and wait for the offers to come flooding in. You need to actively scan the ads and respond promptly for consideration. Some ads will linger for weeks while others are posted and filled very quickly.

My experience with these sites has not been entirely positive. I have found that newspaper ads seem to carry with them a much higher sense of urgency. When an employer places and ad in a newspaper they are expecting immediate response and have resources in place to process respondents. Oftentimes it seems as though no one at the other end is paying any attention to the online ads.

Some sites, such as jobs.washingtonpost.com, are actually online postings of ads placed in the newspapers. While this medium will allow you to peruse ads on your computer, my preference is to plow through the good old Sunday paper using the system outlined above.

Interviewing Success

So, you've responded to a zillion ads and now you're beginning to get calls to come in for interviews. Gulp! Now what do you do?

In researching this book I came across a great short article by a woman named Pat Schuler who makes the analogy of a person preparing for an interview (sales or employment) being like a pilot preparing to take off in a plane. Pat's point is that being well prepared is half the battle.

> *Before a pilot takes off, she walks around the plane with a checklist and does a pre-flight inspection. She checks things off as she completes them. Are you having interviews (phone or in person) for which you are not prepared? Do you go to a networking meeting or an informational*

interview without specific questions and objectives in mind?

You may be saying, "I'm not a pilot. What's the big deal?" Well, if you flub an interview, do you want it to be for something unanticipated or because you didn't take the time to prepare in advance? Yes, if you're late for an interview because you didn't confirm directions, no one dies. Securing a new position isn't life and death. Sometimes it just feels like it.

Take a tip from top performing salespeople and create your own pre-flight checklist. Yes, many of these things are common sense, but you'd be amazed how many people leave them to chance and as a result, make a less than stellar impression.

Sample items for your pre-flight checklist:

Research on company and industry

Polished shoes

Pressed clothing

Good grooming

Appropriate clothing for the position

Confirmed directions

Resume and cover letter you sent

Your ideal job list

Your strengths

Leave 20 minutes earlier than your worst-case estimate

Your weaknesses converted to strengths

Healthy breakfast

Good sleep previous night

Role-plays for tough questions

Your goal for the meeting

Your call to action question

Car gassed up

No stops en route

If you experience a situation that makes you less effective than you'd like for the interview or meeting, add the preventative measure to your pre-flight list. You appear more professional and in control. By preparing in advance for those areas you can control, you leave yourself more leeway to deal with the unexpected.

More sage advice from Pat Schuler can be found at gemini-pro.com, the web site for Pat's company, The Gemini Resources Group.

Getting To The Church On Time

So, following Pat's advice, you've arrived at the interview site twenty minutes early. Do you go right in? Heavens no! You've only assured yourself that you will not be late to a very important meeting. Like the interviewer, your time is valuable; so don't go into the reception area any earlier than ten minutes prior to the appointed hour.

Ten minutes will give you enough time to navigate any pesky express elevators, missing receptionists, unexpected delays at security checkpoints, etc. and still show up right on time. If you are a few moments early you may find that you need the time to fill out a questionnaire handed to you by the receptionist.

This is one of many reasons it is a great idea to have with you a copy of the same resume and cover letter you sent this employer. Much of the questionnaire may cover information contained in your resume, and you want to be sure that both documents match up.

The presence of such a questionnaire may indicate that the company is interviewing a large number of candidates and wants to have a common yardstick of their own making to use when comparing and contrasting – and just plain trying to remember who each person was – further into the selection process. Don't let it throw you.

The Waiting Game

Now you are in one of the toughest spots in this whole difficult process: waiting in the reception area. You can feel the sweat dripping from your armpits. You wonder if your face is flushed. Strange little itches keep cropping up on the top of your head and the back of your neck. The receptionist seems to be smirking at you. After all, she already works here. Again, don't let it throw you.

Just as with sales calls, one of the biggest confidence builders you can have here is the knowledge that this is just one of many calls that you will be making as you market yourself. It is also helpful to remember that you are not there to beg for a job but rather to see if there is a potential match between the requirements they have and the skills you bring. Your presence and offering are valuable. Both parties are investing time and energy into the meeting.

Speaking of time, don't allow your interviewer to keep you waiting. Whether on a sales call or an employment interview, I would not wait more than twenty minutes beyond the appointed time – unless I felt that there were reasonable extenuating circumstances preventing my host from meeting with me. I would also have to have the additional time available to wait *and* conduct a reasonable interview. If not I would move on.

Operate from a position of strength. If it is now fifteen minutes past and you have neither seen nor heard anything from your interviewer, ask the receptionist to check with him to see if you should return another day. If the answer is not to your satisfaction, wait another five minutes and then graciously tell the receptionist that you are working on a very tight schedule and wanted to allot a respectable amount of time to the interview. Thank her for her time and tell her you will call back to reschedule.

This is not going to help you get the job but the chances are that someone who has left you waiting for twenty minutes without so much as a call to the front desk is not someone you want to work for anyway. If they do not call you back to apologize and reschedule, then you can make your own decision whether you would like to do so yourself. Unless this is a company and offering you really think is exceptional, my advice would be to move on. There are just too many great opportunities out there to put up with this.

The Handshake

Assuming that you haven't already walked out in disgust, there will come a point where your interviewer will arrive at the reception area to greet you. Here comes another biggie: The Initial Handshake.

Everyone has their own opinion on how best to handle a handshake. The most important point is to realize that it is worth some consideration. There are few other circumstances under which you will actually be touching someone you don't know in such a direct manner. Do you want your touch to be perceived as cold? Clammy? Weak? Unnecessarily strong and overbearing? I don't.

As the interviewer I came to expect that just about every person I was going to meet would be nervous and, as a result, their handshakes may be hot and sweaty – as opposed to dry, or cold and clammy. You can't help what the surface temperature and relative humidity of your palm will be at the moment of truth, but you can be sure to make the overall impression of your handshake positive.

For me, the best possible handshake is one where I present my hand, look the other person directly in the eye and say "I'm Frank Felker. Good to meet you" as I firmly grasp their hand. Once you have given the other person the chance to respond in kind, you release their hand. Your grip should be firm and confident but not bone crushing. You are trying to present yourself as sincere, not invincible.

With these two nerve-wracking prerequisites (The Wait and The Handshake) out of the way, you're ready to get down to business.

The Interview

Again following the sales call analogy, you want to spend a couple of moments doing what is known as the warm-up. This is a short period of small talk which allows both people to get a feel for the other's mood and personality. If the interviewer has already begun that process, go with it; be yourself, answer questions, pose light questions of your own regarding the weather, something you saw on your way in, etc. Don't get into anything too heavy regarding the job, company or anything else yet.

The objective of the warm-up is to get a feel for the person you are dealing with, a frame of reference within which you can process his questions and formulate your responses. Is this person highly conservative, unemotional and stiff or is he flamboyant, expressive and possibly capable of sudden bursts of temper? You wouldn't present to both of these personalities the same way.

It is also important to try to decipher the difference between his overriding personality and his current mood. An apparently sullen individual may normally be very sunny and fun to talk to but has recently had a difficult experience in his personal life. Spend whatever time seems appropriate getting to know your interlocutor before getting down to brass tacks.

Reading people is an extremely important skill for a successful salesperson, and the sooner you start learning how to do it, the faster you will become adept at it. My read of people is not always correct, but I reflect upon and learn from my mistakes and get better each time. My approach is to start out conservatively and then open up more as I sense openness in the other person. You can always tell a joke later, but you can never un-say words you wish you hadn't spoken earlier.

The transition from warm-up to interview can be awkward, so be sure to let the interviewer handle it. As soon as the two of you sit down you should hand them the copy of your resume and cover letter you brought with you. The odds are that they will not have a copy with them and will appreciate you bringing one for them while noting your level of preparedness.

Again you should allow the interviewer to take the lead. If she is worth her salt she will be prepared to tell you a little about the company and the job you are applying for - possibly even a written job description for you to review. She should also have a list of questions in front of her that she is asking all of the candidates along with a few specifically for you based upon your resume.

Don't be surprised or unprepared though if the interviewer simply sits down and says "So, how can I help you today." This is a quick way to test a prospective salesperson's ability to react to an unexpected situation and sell themselves. The best way to handle this is to express your gratitude for them meeting with you, your enthusiasm for the opportunity to work for their company and your desire to ask her a few questions about the position. You would then begin asking her appropriate questions from the list I have provided below.

Another tactic a Type-A sales manager may employ is to boldly come out and say, "Why should I hire you for this job?" Again, this is done in an attempt to knock you off your feet and see how you pick yourself up, dust yourself off and pitch right back at her.

My response to this question would be to refuse to rise to the bait by answering, "I'm not sure that you should. We don't really know enough about each other yet to see if we have a match here. May I ask you a few questions about your company and the position you have available?" If the interviewer smiles and engages with you then you've impressed him or her with your chutzpah. If they get indignant, you're probably meeting with someone you don't want to work for anyway.

The usual course of events is the first one: the interviewer leads the conversation with an overview of the company and the job description, and then asks you a series of questions about yourself and your qualifications. At whatever point he is finished, he will either ask you if you have any questions for him or say, "Well, thanks very much for coming in. We'll be in touch." He may also say "Wow! You're the best candidate we've seen for this position! When can you start?" In either case your response again should be, "May I ask you a few questions first?"

Qualifying Questions

Don't kid yourself: you may not want this job. Remember your personal priorities regarding income potential, risk aversion, travel, etc. Whether you are on a sales call or an employment interview, you need to find out if your prospect is qualified to receive what you have to offer.

Asking questions and listening closely to the answers is the primary tactic of any true sales professional. As I've stated before, sales is not something you do to someone, it's something you do for them. Find out what they are looking for, what they really need, and figure out if you can bring it to them.

In addition to helping you qualify this company as a prospective employer, the questions below will also position you as a savvy, revenue-focused sales professional. An experienced manager will pick up on the fact that you are looking for a business opportunity, not a handout.

One word of caution about questioning your interviewer: don't come on too strong. The last thing you want to do is put him on the defensive by coming across as overly nosey, pushy or judgmental. You may even wish to delay asking some or all of these questions until a second interview if you feel one is in the offing. No matter what, ask the lighter questions first and then ease into the stronger ones, as you feel appropriate. Focus on their business first and your compensation second. And stop asking if you get the sense that the other person is becoming upset.

Your Question List

Tell me what kind of customers you would want me to bring in. Describe your best customer.

(Make sure they understand that you are not asking them to name their best customer, but rather to describe that customer's attributes: what industry they are in, how big is the company, how long have they been buying from you, what makes them so great?)

Who are some clients you'd love to land?

What kinds of customers do you want me to avoid?

Are there any particular product lines that we are trying to push right now?

Who will I be competing against?

Does the company provide qualified leads or are the salespeople expected to do the majority of their own prospecting?

What is generally the title of the decision-maker at targeted companies?

How long is the usual sales cycle?

What are our normal payment terms?

Do we offer in-house financing?

Tell me about your most successful salesperson? How long have they been with the company? What do they do that sets them apart? What do you wish they would do differently?

How did this job come available? What happened to the last person? How long has this position been in existence?

Is there a written job description?

What sort of training do you offer?

How will my performance be evaluated? How often? By whom?

What is the range of income potential with this job?

In this industry, what are the most common objections and what are the best overcomes?

How much travel is required for this job?

What sort of advertising and marketing support and collateral do you provide?

How does your compensation plan work?

Are your salespeople W-2 employees or 1099 sub-contractors?

What sort of benefits package do you offer?

What is the company's policy regarding holidays, sick days and paid vacation?

Asking all or most of these questions will assure your interviewer that you are serious about your sales career. And their responses will go a long way to let you know if you want the job they are offering.

Once you are done with your questioning be sure to tell them with something like, "Well, those are all the questions I have for right now." This is a clear signal to them that it is time for them to wrap up the meeting.

The Trial Close

As I mentioned earlier, there is an expression in sales that goes "Always Be Closing," also known as the ABCs of Sales. In sales, the verb "to close" refers to consummating the sale. All the prospecting and presenting in the world is useless unless somebody signs a contract and delivers a check. As a result, closing is the ultimate objective in sales and one should Always Be Closing.

There are a million closing techniques but the one I recommend here is The Trial Close. In other words, as you are getting up from the table you come right out and ask your interviewer, "So, do I have the job?" You can be sure that will get a rise out of him.

Any good sales manager will be pleasantly surprised by this question. He probably isn't ready to give the job to anyone yet but will definitely remember you. As he hems and haws and avoids a direct answer to your direct question you can let him off the hook by laughing and asking him how you did in the interview and what your overall chances are to get the job. No matter what, you want to get a clear next-step response.

If he tells you that he still has five candidates to interview, ask him when that process will be completed and what he will do once it is. If he hasn't already told you, ask him how many resumes he received and how many people he is interviewing. Ask him if he will contact you or if you should call him back on a date certain.

Even if you don't want the job, you should use this opportunity to practice your assertiveness and closing techniques. Whatever you do, don't leave there without either a definite "no thank you" from him or a specific action plan regarding what is to happen next.

The Post-Interview Recap

After each interview take a few minutes in your car in the parking lot to review in your mind what just happened. Did you present as well as you had hoped? What questions were you asked that you weren't prepared for? Did you read your interviewer well or make a major faux pas? What should you add to your pre-flight list to be better prepared for your next interview? Your time is valuable, so you want to make the most of everything you put into the preparation, travel and meetings. If you can do better the next time, be sure you do.

Choosing The Right Opportunity

The final step in this whole harangue is deciding which job to take. Clearly there is no one correct answer and I wouldn't presume to tell you what is right for you, your career and your family. But there are a number of points we have touched on previously that you would do well to revisit now as you make a final decision.

First off, it isn't a final decision. This first sales job may only be a stepping-stone to one or more additional opportunities down the road. You definitely should pick something that you are willing to commit to for at least twelve months, but don't base your decision on which job you want to do for the rest of your life. The best first sales job might be the one that offers the best training, biggest safety net of base pay and benefits with a well-established, financially strong company.

Be sure to revisit your personal priorities of income potential, downside risk and travel requirements. Maybe you'd be willing to travel for the next couple of years to make the money you need to give you a stronger foundation for another job later. If you're a young person, possibly just out of college or the military and living at home with your folks, you might be willing to take a flyer on a high-risk, all-commission job that offers unbelievable income potential.

As for the offering, there is only one thing you need to be sure of: that you believe in it. Your level of industry-specific knowledge is not nearly as important as your belief that this product or service is something great. You want to represent a product that everyone would want if they only knew about it. Belief in your product will see you through virtually every challenge you meet in selling it.

As for the company; this may be the hardest decision of all. You can love the product and be comfortable with the compensation plan and travel schedule but absolutely hate the people you're working with. Unfortunately there is no way to know that until you've been on the inside for a while. One benefit with sales is that you will probably be spending the majority of your time away from the office. Again, you must be committed to hanging in there at least a year – even if the people stink.

Just like neighbors and family members, co-workers are a matter of fate. In some cases corporate culture plays a part in what type of people you will work with but, for the most part, it's just dumb luck. Reconcile yourself to the fact that you won't know who you'll be working with no matter which job you choose.

More important considerations revolve around the ownership, history, reputation, management and financial stability of the company you join. Wherever possible, choose the older company with the deeper pockets that has the best track record – especially for your first foray into sales. You can always take a flyer on the high-risk, high-return start-up company once you've earned your bones. Pick one and give it your best shot.

Conclusion:
Now It's Your Turn

I sincerely hope that you have enjoyed and found value in this book. I have tried to make it as complete an introduction to the opportunities available in a sales career as possible without delving too deeply into individual details. Only you can tell me how well I have succeeded at that.

Now it's time for action. If you are sincere in your desire to change your circumstances, find career satisfaction and build financial independence for yourself and your family, you have everything you need to get started. But only you can make it happen.

Start perusing the classifieds, brush-up your resume, determine the offerings and companies that appeal to you and start responding to ads. It's never too late and it's never too soon to take charge of your situation and make it happen.

Remember: this is not a get-rich-quick scheme. You are pursuing a new career direction which requires commitment and hard work. But it doesn't require specialized technical training, a college degree, a family pedigree or previous experience - in either sales or the industry you enter.

Anyone can succeed at sales. Whether you will or not depends entirely on your belief in yourself and your offering.

In addition to writing this book I have also read it several times as part of the editing process. The experience reminds me very much of producing original music in a recording studio. You hear the same song over and over so many times that it becomes almost impossible to try to perceive it the way a first-time listener might.

As a first-time reader of this book you bring a fresh perspective and pair of eyes that I cannot. It is for that reason that your feedback is greatly appreciated.

As part of the proofreading and editing process I distributed draft copies to a number of people who are already in the sales game. Their response surprised me and leads me to believe that there may be a market for this information among existing sales professionals in addition to those looking for a new way to make a living.

The edition you are reading is the first of what I hope will be many printings. With experience in both printing and marketing, it made sense for me to self-publish. Initially I am printing relatively small runs using digital technology. If demand dictates I will use more traditional book printing and binding methods for larger runs going forward. No matter what, I will be making additions and corrections with each printing.

With that in mind I encourage you to tell me of any oversights, misstatements, typographical errors or other mistakes you found as you read the book. Email them to me at comments@thegreatestjob.com I will do my best to make sure the corrections are incorporated into the next edition.

Thank you very much for your time and patronage. I hope you will be reading another of my books in the near future.

Frank Felker

> "The starting point of
> all achievement is desire."
>
> Napoleon Hill

Quick Order Form

Fax Orders: 707-202-1754. Send this form

Telephone Orders: Call toll-free 1-866-390-1945. Have your credit card ready.

Email Orders: orders@powerhousepublishing.com

Web Orders: www.TheGreatestJob.com/choose_product.html

Postal Orders: Powerhouse Publishing, 9538 Old Keene Mill Road, #324, Burke, VA 22015-4208, USA. Telephone 703-644-0704

Please send the following copies/editions of The Greatest Job You Never Thought Of

_____	Hardcover Books @ $26.95 =	$ _____
_____	Paperback Books @ $14.95 =	$ _____
_____	4-CD Audio Books @ $34.95 =	$ _____
_____	1-CD MP3 Audio Books @ $14.95 =	$ _____
_____	1-CD Electronic Books @ $14.95 =	$ _____
	Sub-total	$ _____
5% Sales Tax on Orders Shipped to Virginia		$ _____
$4.99 Ground Shipping and Handling		$ _____
	Total	$ _____

Name: _____

Address: _____

City: _____ State: _____ Zip: _____

Email Address: _____

Payment: Cheque   Credit Card

                          Visa   MasterCard

Card Number: _____

Name on Card: _____

Exp. Date: _____ Verification Number: _____

Please send me more information on:

   Bulk Purchases   Speaking/Seminars   Consulting

"Our doubts are traitors, and make us lose the good we oft might win, by fearing to attempt."

William Shakespeare

Quick Order Form

POWER HOUSE
PUBLISHING

Fax Orders: 707-202-1754. Send this form

Telephone Orders: Call toll-free 1-866-390-1945. Have your credit card ready.

Email Orders: orders@powerhousepublishing.com

Web Orders: www.TheGreatestJob.com/choose_product.html

Postal Orders: Powerhouse Publishing, 9538 Old Keene Mill Road, #324, Burke, VA 22015-4208, USA. Telephone 703-644-0704

Please send the following copies/editions of The Greatest Job You Never Thought Of:

_____	Hardcover Books @ $26.95 =	$ _____
_____	Paperback Books @ $14.95 =	$ _____
_____	4-CD Audio Books @ $34.95 =	$ _____
_____	1-CD MP3 Audio Books @ $14.95 =	$ _____
_____	1-CD Electronic Books @ $14.95 =	$ _____
	Sub-total	$ _____
	5% Sales Tax on Orders Shipped to Virginia	$ _____
	$4.99 Ground Shipping and Handling	$ _____
	Total	$ _____

Name: _____

Address: _____

City: _____ **State:** _____ **Zip:** _____

Email Address: _____

Payment: Cheque   Credit Card

                              Visa   MasterCard

Card Number: _____

Name on Card: _____

Exp. Date: _____ **Verification Number:** _____

Please send me more information on:

   Bulk Purchases   Speaking/Seminars   Consulting

618347

Made in the USA